From the files of the National Enquirer

FREAK!

Inside the twisted world of Michael Jackson

By
Nick Bishop

American Media Inc.

From the files of the National Enquirer:
FREAK! Inside the twisted world of Michael Jackson

Copyright © 2003 AMI Books, Inc.

Cover design: Imageblast
Interior design: Debbie Duckworth
Cover photographs: Michael Jackson in court — Ramey Photo Agency; Michael Jackson with baby in window — Landov

ISBN: 1-885840-05-5

First printing: February 2003

Printed in the United States of America

10 9 8 7 6 5 4 3 2 1

freak \frēk\ *n*: a person or animal on exhibition as an example of a strange deviation from nature; a monster.

— Webster's Dictionary

On Tuesday, November 19, 2002, Michael Jackson was in Germany to attend a benefit for homeless children. He had volunteered to place a few personal items on the auction block for the philanthropic cause and made it a point to announce, as he always did, that there was nothing more important to him than the welfare of children. He understood children — and they understood him. Nobody loved children more than Michael Jackson.

Some 200 enthusiastic fans had gathered outside the Adlon Hotel in Berlin, screaming and holding banners, hoping for a glimpse of Michael. The golden voice of Motown still echoed through the internal speakers of aging supporters who remembered the magic of yesteryear. It was a far cry from the crowds the fallen superstar once attracted. The most popular entertainer in the music industry with the best-selling album ever, Thriller, had not been packing them in as he once did. A lot had gone down since his successful glory days during the '70s and '80s.

In fact, things had been getting ugly, of late — very ugly. Michael's face is literally falling apart, the years of plastic surgery leaving a once handsome man painfully disfigured. It is as if no media outlet can run a photo of him now without seeking comment from psychologists to answer the obvious question that arises, "Why?" The face, if you can call it that, has been bleached white, even whiter than white, and is caked with makeup on top of that. There's nothing even left of his nose to repair, often seen bandaged and infected.

Michael, in his better days, was a man obsessed with freaks. He tried to buy the Elephant Man's bones and collected human brains in formaldehyde. He even once kept a piece of his own nose (removed in one of the many surgeries) in his bedroom at home, a memento of sorts. He became an expert on abnormal phenomena and his favorite movie was E.T. He claims to have watched the flick end to end over 500 times. Michael always said that he identified with the outcast and the exploited. It had something to do with his own lost childhood and innocence, from his own youth lost to performing for others.

Michael had long cultivated a bizarre image — sleeping in a hyperbaric chamber in hopes of living to be 150, releasing photos with the contingency that the word "bizarre" even be used. It seems as if he hung out only with little boys, or his "special friends" as he called them. Then there was his pet monkey, Bubbles. He dressed the animal in matching outfits to his own, held its hand, and cuddled up in public to the furry friend.

Everything childish became his obsession, from building an amusement park called Neverland on his own estate, to pillow and water balloon fights. Once again, it was all about the children for Michael, the only people who really understood and didn't judge him.

But now, tragically, it was all coming back to haunt him. The drug abuse, including reports of regular IV drips of the highly potent painkiller Demerol, was out of control. The failing career, with rumors of impending bankruptcy, was hard for a man who once inked a billion-dollar record contract with Sony Music. And worst of all, those stories of pedophilia Michael was never able to shake. Once the father of Jordie Chandler showed up in 1993, accusing the superstar of molesting his son, things really fell apart. The man once obsessed with freaks had himself become one.

So Michael liked to hang out with little boys more than anyone else. So he liked to shower them with gifts, run amok in toy stores after hours and give them whatever their hearts desired. So what if he liked to have them spend the night in his secret playroom, he and the little boys snuggling together in the same bed and watching E.T. on the television? He had managed to foster such relationships with countless little boys before Jordie Chandler. He showered impressionable families with money, and the parents left him and the boys alone to play their games in peace. He was a god to these little boys, he was their savior, and nobody cared more about children than Michael Jackson.

Facing a criminal investigation, it was reported that Michael elected to pay Jordie Chandler $20 million to make the whole thing go away. There were rumors that there were two other boys that might be talking to authorities, as well. Employees were starting to speak out, and even his sister LaToya held a press conference to say she had seen him sneaking little boys into their parents' home when he was in his late teens and 20s. According to Michael, it was all a big misunderstanding. He had been humiliated, and it was an outrage, he announced on CNN. Once again, he insisted, nobody cared more about children than Michael Jackson.

So he married Lisa Marie Presley to try to repair the damage, and even gave her a passionate kiss on national television. For hours he practiced that kiss on a mannequin in his dressing room before the big event. It was important that the entire thing looked natural, that he was a regular Romeo. Everyone would see that he was into women — not little boys. That marriage lasted less than two years, and still to this day, people wonder how much he had to pay her to keep quite about their so-called "sex life."

Once again, Michael had to save his image, marrying his dermatologist's assistant, Debbie Rowe. Reports surfaced that he had her artificially inseminated and then, after she served as little more than an incubator for his prodigy, he whisked the children away from her before she could even touch them, whispering, "Don't get too attached." No one, after all, could care for children as well as Michael.

Michael paid Debbie Rowe a million dollars for each baby she bore him, and millions more to maintain the marriage. She played along, insisting he was a red-blooded man, a stud, anything but a pedophile child molester! He dressed up like a pirate, like Peter Pan, according to Debbie Rowe, and then there was no stopping him. Even so, in the end, she divorced him. Even the reported millions she would receive wasn't enough to keep her following his simple rules!

Then things got even worse for the King of Pop. His latest album, Invincible, tanked, and even though Sony Music spent $30 million to produce it, it had to be their fault. Michael, a black man who had been doing everything in his power to turn white over the years, screamed racism. It was a conspiracy against black artists, bringing him down, and Sony should pay.

By the end of 2002, just before arriving in Berlin, Jackson had even been hauled into a California courtroom. He had to testify in a $21 million lawsuit filed against him, claiming he backed out of scheduled millennium concerts.

But still, throughout it all, Jackson professed a love for children, and most of all, for his own. In an address recently at Oxford University, he announced, "I pray that my children will say to themselves 'our daddy did the best he could . . . He may not have been perfect, but he was a warm and decent man, who tried to give us all the love in the world'."

Grinning from ear to ear that November day

in Berlin, Michael stepped from his hotel room wearing a bright red shirt and waving enthusiastically to his fans. He was still popular and loved. For a moment, he forgot his troubles.

Michael turned suddenly, went back inside, and retrieved the youngest of his three children, Prince Michael II. The baby had simply been introduced as "Number 3" a few months beforehand, with little explanation about his parentage. Was he Michael's biological child? Had Debbie Rowe been employed to carry another Jackson? Or was he adopted?

Holding the infant with one arm, Jackson emerged, focused more on holding a towel over the baby's face than anything else. Whenever he appeared with his children out in public he insisted in veiling their appearances. The very next day, he would go to the zoo with the older kids, Prince Michael I and Paris, covered in purple netting. But that Jackson freak show paled in relation to what happened on the balcony of the Adlon hotel.

Jackson dangled Prince Michael II over the railing — 65 feet up — swaying him back and forth. The helpless baby, dressed in a baby-blue sleeper and barefoot, started squirming and struggling as his father fought to keep control and, at one point, seemed to nearly lose his grip. Twice, he knocked the child's legs on the railings. Michael finally took the baby between his legs, hauled him back to safety and retreated into his suite.

For the few Michael Jackson fans left, it was the last straw. In one ultimate irony, Wacko Jacko, in town to help children, had nearly killed his very own.

"The world sees me as this monstrous freak who abuses little boys." — Michael Jackson to Elizabeth Taylor, as reported in *Michael Jackson: Unauthorized.*

CHAPTER 1

It is a hot August day in 2002, and the lighting in the penthouse suite is nightclub dim. Michael Jackson sits on the sofa dressed all in black, slippers with rhinestone studs on his feet and sunglasses covering his eyes. His complexion, already pale, is smeared with white makeup. He has some kind of peach fuzz on his face. It isn't a beard exactly, not a 5 o'clock shadow, but more like some weird and unsuccessful hybrid of the scruffy look. It doesn't come off right, one editor describes.

Jackson informs the visiting publishers that he is set to write another book. When he did *Moonwalk* with Jackie O, he explains, he really wasn't ready to talk. Jackie had twisted his arm. Now he will set the record straight. He has been misunderstood, slandered and vilified. He is, he assures his audience, a regular guy. He will counter the lies and distortions and clear his reputation once and for all.

Then Jackson suddenly bursts into tears, crying

quietly on the sofa while the publishers wait in silence for him to resume his pitch, but he withdraws into a ball, trying to make himself smaller.

On The Jacksons tour in 1981 for the Triumph album, he would disappear in a tremendous puff of smoke at the conclusion of singing his showstopping number "Don't Stop 'Til You Get Enough."

Now, it's as if he wants to relive those glory days, to turn back the clock, and to go out at the top of his game.

When he had met Shirley Temple, Jackson manages to compose himself long enough to explain, she asked if he was disappointed in her. He elaborates on how this legendary child star, like himself, sacrificed her youth to entertain others. Now, when fans meet her, she told him it is as though she has let them down somehow by growing up. They wanted her to remain a cute little kid forever. So, naturally, she had wondered aloud if Michael felt disappointed in meeting her, too.

The truth is, he harbors only compassion — he feels so isolated, he admits, that sometimes he goes up to complete strangers and asks them to be his friend.

On August 28, 2002, Michael Jackson held court in the Westin Hotel in Stamford, Connecticut, a city some 60 miles northeast of New York City. In years past, Michael used to take over sumptuous suites at places like the Waldorf-Astoria or Trump

Tower, smack in the core of the Big Apple. This time, he was relegated to the suburbs.

He was "in town"— though 60 miles out of it — for two reasons. First, he had been lured to the MTV Music Awards ceremony to be held at Radio City Music Hall, where he was to receive an award as The Entertainer of the Millennium. Second, he was hawking a book on his life that he hoped would set the record straight.

Twenty years earlier, Jackson came to New York riding a crest of unrivaled popularity. He was there to sell his first autobiography for several million dollars. He succeeded and, in a fitting touch, had for his editor the most publicized woman in history, none other than Jacqueline Kennedy Onassis.

The book was called *Moonwalk* and it became a huge international best seller. Fans of Michael Jackson had to have a copy, and they numbered in the millions worldwide. *Moonwalk* rode the top of the charts for months. In terms of spin, the book was masterful, presenting a fairy-tale image of Michael Jackson as a trouble-free young man possessed of talent at the level of genius. His heart was larger than life and his compassion inexhaustible — especially when it came to children. Where children were concerned, he was a veritable masked crusader, striving to set right every wrong.

Moonwalk outlined the Jackson legend. It recounted how the children of a large but economically challenged African-American working class family in Gary, Indiana, catapulted their way to international fame as the Jackson 5 in the late '60s

and early '70s. They worked themselves to the bone
to achieve the pinnacle of the pop music world,
sacrificing comfort and sleep to travel in a van
hundreds of miles to compete endlessly in amateur
competitions, distinguishing themselves along the
way with victory after victory. They were lucky to
have a father, himself an amateur musician, who had
the vision to shape the talents of his children. Their
act, even in the early stages, was polished beyond
their years.

In *Moonwalk*, Michael told of their 1968 tryout
with Berry Gordy's Motown Records, now a part of
American folklore and legend. Gordy was a god to
aspiring black singers, songwriters and entertainers
in the '60s, '70s and '80s. There went the Jacksons,
off in their family van for the five-hour trip through
the night to Detroit and the audition with Motown.
Mother Katherine Jackson had packed them
sandwiches. Father Joe was at the wheel. They got to
Detroit, caught forty winks in a hotel, rose the
next morning and performed for Mr. Gordy with all
they had.

Joe Jackson and his sons drove the lonely
stretches of interstate back to Gary not knowing
whether they had caught the big break or crapped
out. Then the call came from Berry Gordy himself.
Father Joe was offered a recording contract for
the musical services of the group composed of his
five sons.

The Jacksons would soon become household
names. Their fans clamored for every tidbit of
information about Jackie, Tito, Jermaine, Marlon
and Michael, the youngest yet the lead singer.

Wherever they went, they were mobbed. Their fame was reminiscent of the Beatles eight years earlier. Police escorted them to and from performance venues with lights flashing and sirens blaring. Hotels where they stayed had to add security. Female fans tried ruses and disguises to get to their rooms.

One year after signing with Motown, the Jackson 5 had their first number one hit on the charts, "I Want You Back." The following year they had four more.

Yet their father, Joe, isolated his sons. It seemed he cut them off from the outside world, except for carefully orchestrated interviews and photo sessions. The image put forth was of a family devoted to each other and dedicated to hard work. They were one big happy family, always pulling together, happiest when they were in each other's company. Their mother, Katherine, was portrayed accurately as a devout Jehovah's Witness whose faith was unshakable, despite having been marked with a limp from a childhood bout with polio. Her closeness to God was portrayed as a cornerstone for the entire family.

When Berry Gordy had signed the Jackson 5, Michael was only 10. Even at that point, he was a veteran of five years in the entertainment business. At age 5, Joe had Michael performing with the group in the family living room of their small and modest house in Gary. He had also been exposed, along with his brothers, to strippers and every other kind of adult entertainment in down and dirty clubs — then shuttled to church on Sunday with his mother and sister. The Jehovah's Witnesses reviled everything these clubs represented. So quickly, for Michael, the fissure opened between reality and fantasy. His personality was split between the profane and the sacred. At night he sang and danced in seamy clubs and by day he knocked on doors and implored people to convert.

In 1972, the year he turned 14, Michael's first solo album hit the charts. That same year, he recorded a song for the soundtrack of the hit movie Ben. The song, called simply "Ben," rocketed up the charts to No. 1 and became the biggest-selling single for Motown in all of the '70s.

In 1976, the Jackson 5 and Motown Records split in an acrimonious showbiz divorce. Because Berry Gordy claimed control of the name the "Jackson 5," when the brothers sang with Epic Records they changed their name to "The Jacksons." By this time, Jermaine Jackson had married Berry Gordy's daughter, Hazel Joy. When Jermaine elected to stay with Motown Records and his new father-in-law, who had promised to make Jermaine a solo star, The Jacksons countered by inserting youngest son Randy in his place. The group boomed along without pause.

The summer of 1976 witnessed the premiere on network television of their family musical variety show, titled simply The Jacksons. It continued on the air into 1977. All eight Jackson children were involved in the show. Only Jermaine, still with the Gordys and Motown, was missing. The Jacksons were at this point the most successful family in the history of American popular music. The key to their success was clearly Michael, quickly morphing into a superstar.

The next year, The Jacksons were so popular that they gave a royal performance in Glasgow, Scotland, at Kings Hall in honor of Queen Elizabeth II. Their worldwide appeal grew and all their concerts were sellouts. They performed to packed stadiums and arenas throughout Asia, Europe and Australia.

In 1979, the same year Michael turned 18, he released the Off the Wall Album. It dazzled music business execs when it went on to sell eight million copies around the world. Michael's hit "Don't Stop 'Til You Get Enough" grabbed the Grammy for Best Single, R&B Male Vocal.

That same year Michael landed his first movie role. He was cast to play the Scarecrow in the Wiz, the adaptation from the Broadway sensation. The film would star Diana Ross, an early sponsor of the Jackson 5 and a kind of surrogate mother and role model for Michael. For his part as the Scarecrow, Michael had to wear an elaborate costume and heavy makeup. In rehearsals, he picked up the dance steps so quickly from the choreographer that the other cast members became jealous.

Although the movie version of the Wiz was not successful, this setback hardly derailed the ascendancy of Michael Jackson. He was about to achieve megastardom in the unforgettable year of 1982, when Thriller was released and went on to be the top-selling album of all time. To date, this album has sold 40 million copies around the world. Nothing like it had ever been seen before.

In an unprecedented move in the record business, Michael produced three videos to tie in with the release of Thriller. He hired director John Landis

(National Lampoon's Animal House and The Blues Brothers) to film the main video. It was the equivalent of a movie short — a full story — with a beginning, a middle, and an end. It featured choreography worthy of Jerome Robbins and West Side Story. Dance sequences were shot in the underground concourse of the Rockefeller Center subway stop in Manhattan. No one had ever spent anything near a million dollars on a video before, as Michael induced Epic Records to do. When the video aired on MTV, it helped sell a million copies of the album each week for a month.

Michael also shot shorter videos to promote the two biggest hits on the Thriller album, "Billie Jean" and "Beat It." By doing this, Michael Jackson galvanized and revolutionized the music business. Soon, every other solo artist and group demanded a video like the one for Thriller. The music video was no longer just another promo gimmick. It sparked the whole music industry and spurred it on to new heights of promotion, all centered on the tie-in video.

Thriller was released at the tailend of 1982. All through 1983 it blasted away at the top of the charts. "Billie Jean" and "Beat It," both written by Michael, became instant pop classics.

Then on Monday, May 16, lightning struck. The TV special called "Motown 25: Yesterday, Today, Forever," aired. The audience was estimated at 50 million viewers and all of them saw Michael Jackson electrify the world. Dressed all in black, with what would become his trademark sequined glove on his right hand and his snow-white socks glistening with sequins above black loafers, he pressed an indelible image on the collective conscience of the 20th century. His "moonwalk" is rivaled in popular entertainment only by Charlie Chaplin's tramp walk, Gene Kelly's Singing in the Rain sequence and Fred Astaire dancing on the walls and ceiling in Royal Wedding.

In turn, the TV special boosted the already roaring sales of Thriller. Articles appeared all over the world extolling Michael Jackson as the most famous entertainer of all time. Teens everywhere started wearing sequined white socks. Michael giggled his way through interviews and said he loved swimming against the fashion stream and coming out on top. Kids from 2 to 82 tried moonwalking. It was a craze unrivaled since the zany days of the Hoola Hoop in the late '50s.

Thriller was so successful that a video was produced titled The Making of Thriller. This was yet another music industry first pioneered by Michael. Until then only full-length blockbuster movies had merited such treatment, and then almost exclusively in book form. Even this documentary cassette went on to sell a million copies. Nothing like the Michael Jackson phenomenon had ever been seen before. Not even Elvis, as a single performer, or the Beatles, as a group, had reached such dizzying heights of celebrity.

At this point, Michael was still living at home with his parents in Encino, in the family mansion called Hayvenhurst. There, security had been beefed up tremendously after fans continued to invade the property, climbing the high fences surrounding the manor house. A closed-circuit television system had to be installed which featured a surveillance camera mounted on a pole 15 feet high. Still, people tried to get to the Jacksons. Mother Katherine was sometimes so annoyed with the invasion on the family's privacy that she wished the Jacksons were back in their modest home on Jackson Street in Gary, Indiana.

Now, at the very height of stardom, an eccentric side to Michael Jackson began to emerge. He went under the knife for the first time, reappearing in public with what would be the first of many nose jobs. And for years he had been obsessed with Disneyland and other amusement parks. He had an insatiable appetite for fantasy worlds. But because of his mushrooming celebrity, he could no longer visit such public places without fans besieging him. His mere presence could cause near riots.

So at Hayvenhurst he spent a small fortune to re-create his favorite ride. He commissioned engineers from Disney to build a smaller version of the famous Pirates of the Caribbean ride in the Magic Kingdom as an addition to the house itself. The Encino property was large enough that Michael also installed a small private zoo with fawns, cockatoos, macaws, a llama named Louis and a boa constrictor called Muscles. In the house itself, Michael kept what would turn out to be the first of many pet chimpanzees, the original Bubbles. He loved to change the baby chimp's diapers and to kiss and cuddle with it.

Michael also started to show an overinterest in things childish, like toys and costumes. He adored having pillow fights or running around with water pistols, and couldn't get enough of video and computer games. He became an avid and early fan of Atari, PacMan and Donkey Kong. He loved games of hide and seek or to play on monkey bars and to climb trees, especially in the company of young boys.

Michael said, early in his career, that he would produce the highest grossing album of all time. With Thriller, he exceeded the top sales of any album in history, and by a wide margin. At the 1984 Grammy Awards, Michael walked off with eight awards, a record accomplishment. But significantly, it wasn't enough. Michael privately vowed he would someday top it. He couldn't get enough.

For the 1984 Grammy Awards Michael dressed in a black type of military jacket, complete with glittering epaulets, sequins, braid work on the sleeves, and a flashy sash. He looked not unlike a toy soldier as he sat between his official date for the ceremony, Brooke Shields, herself a beautiful child star, and another child star, tiny actor Emmanuel Lewis, the lead character in the hit TV series Webster.

Official date Brooke Shields would later state that Michael showed no romantic interest in her. He did not respond to her attempts to kiss him. On the other hand, he was highly attentive to, and solicitous of, Emmanuel Lewis, very much a youngster. In fact,

Emmanuel Lewis was still a small boy in 1984. Was it possible that Brooke Shields was simply a beard for Michael, a sexual trophy intended to divert attention from his true interest?

———

At the apex of fame, Michael was asked in an interview if he was happy. He replied that he did not believe that he was ever completely happy. He said, in the time-honored fashion of all true artists, that he came closest to being really satisfied when he created and performed. When he put his heart and soul into something and it pleased others — that was what gave him a thrill.

In the years that followed the astonishing personal and professional triumphs of 1984, Michael Jackson flourished. He never succeeded in topping the sales of Thriller, but in January of 1985, he used his influence to organize countless stars of the music world to come together and record his song "We Are the World," Michael's genuine and altruistic response to the horror of children dying of starvation in Africa. The galaxy of stars he assembled was breathtaking. No one else in the world could have pulled it off.

At the 1986 Grammy Awards, "We Are the World" won Song of the Year. Two years later, his autobiography *Moonwalk* became an instant best seller worldwide. Two years later, Michael yet again proved his artistry at producing trendsetting videos when "Leave Me Alone" (from his "Bad" album) won the Grammy for Best Music Video: Short Form.

Late in the following year, Dangerous was released, but the title would prove ironic and prophetic. A little over a year later, in early 1993, while Michael was still on his world tour promoting the album, all hell broke loose. The father of a 13-year-old Los Angeles boy accused Michael of sexually molesting his young son.

Worldwide, Michael Jackson, the most famous entertainer of the 20th century, was publicized as facing charges of pedophilia, and the floodgates of accusation opened against him.

"I am thoroughly bored with myself."
— Michael Jackson pitching a new book to visiting publishers, August 28, 2002.

CHAPTER 2

During his spiel to visiting New York City book publishers on that hot August day in Stamford, Connecticut, in 2002, Michael Jackson appeared disoriented. He would ask the publishers what company they were from. They answered him for a second or third time. This would be doubly odd because the publishers had handed Michael sample promotional materials and their latest catalogs. The names of the companies were clearly visible on all of this.

As Michael's attention drifted away, one publisher tried to refocus him by asking if he exercised.

"I hate exercise," he replied. "I really don't do anything."

"How can you say that," the publisher countered. "You have to be in fabulous shape to do your dance routines and to burn such energy during your performances."

Michael sighed and said, "When I have to perform, I get in shape. I work out fourteen hours a day."

With each publishing group, Michael spoke with

sadness of his loneliness. He said that he barely keeps
in touch with his family and that they rarely get
together. Jehovah's Witnesses do not believe in
holidays, so there are no traditional family gatherings
for the Jacksons. There had been mention, he would
say, of plans for a reunion in Hawaii. There had also
been talk of the entire family going on a camping
expedition. At this prospect, Michael always rolled
his eyes.

Michael worked into the discussion that he had no
friends among his contemporaries. He would cite the
older cadre of Liz Taylor, Liza Minnelli and Marlon
Brando. Ironically, he never mentioned his habit of
keeping company with preadolescent boys and child
stars like Emmanuel Lewis and Macaulay Culkin.
He illustrated for the publishers how tough it was to
be Michael Jackson. He could not go anywhere he
pleased like a normal person. Recently in Las Vegas,
he and Chris Tucker decided to leave their suite and
go down on the gaming floor. That's when the awful
thing happened, the awful thing that always
happened.

"It was terrifying," Michael said in a soft, sad and
wistful voice. "People had to touch me. They had to
keep coming up to me and touching me. Other than
the pope, I'm the most recognizable man in the
world."

Michael would go on to say that he was extremely
uncomfortable with the press. He didn't want
publicity, just to write a real book to set the record
straight and "clear up" misunderstandings. He had
tried to do this years ago with the infamous Diane
Sawyer interview on ABC's Primetime, but he felt

that Sawyer let him down, even though the perception in the rest of the media was the exact opposite.

In the wake of the accusations of child molestation against Michael, Diane Sawyer and ABC were roundly criticized for allowing him to use them as mere flacks to get his own spin out to the public. Others accused the network of cutting a deal with the star to get an exclusive interview, a total rarity, simply to boost their ratings. The Primetime interview was widely considered a whitewash.

Even so, Michael explained that he still feels to this day that Diane Sawyer let him down by not annihilating any hint that he was ever guilty of pedophilia. How could anyone even think such a thing, he would ask rhetorically of the gathered publishers. He, Michael Jackson, loved children, everyone knew that. He couldn't do enough for them. His many gifts of money and time to charities and groups aiding children were a matter of public record.

Rambling with the wind, Jackson would start to explain how he loved his own children more than he could say. But it was hard to raise them. Why? Because they had everything, he declared. And on top of having everything, his friends in show business gave his children even more — even more than everything.

What seemed illogical to others made perfect sense to Michael, and as he fought back tears, the stories continued.

Jackson insisted he was nothing but a regular guy. All else written about him to the contrary was false.

Of course, he told his guests, he does have edge. He said he has always thought and acted outside the box. But first and foremost, he is a regular guy, not the Elephant Man. He had been fascinated by freaks all of his life, but he himself is not one.

Jackson described going up to kids and asking them who they would go to see if they had a choice between Prince and Lionel Richie. He asked them, given a choice, who would you want to see? Whose music would you rather hear? Michael said that they always want to hear Richie. This confirmed his theory that regular guys are preferred. Much like Lionel Richie, he, Michael Jackson, is a regular guy from Gary, Indiana, and so he, too, is preferred by kids.

When the spirit moved him, Michael would let the publishers in on another plan. He wanted to write at least one book for children. It was an obsession — even to this day he loved to read children's books. He was practically addicted to them. When he was living at Hayvenhurst he had a whole library of children's literature in his bedroom, and he read those books all the time. He didn't have to tell his visitors, for they all knew, that he was crazy about children. But he told them this anyway.

If he wrote the first children's book and it was successful, he intended to write many more. He would become a children's book writer and parents would naturally flock to his books. They would buy them for their children with enthusiasm. After all, they would be written by one of the world's foremost entertainers and a man whose charity toward children was celebrated the world over.

The children's book he planned would be as well meaning and as wholesome as his song "Heal the World." He intended to use the same sensibility in the children's book that he used to create this altruistic and award-winning song that had done so much to benefit the poor and starving children around the world, especially in Africa and Asia.

His name on children's literature would be magical. It would be a kind of seal of approval. It would lend distinction.

Three years after Moonwalk hit the best-seller lists, Michael's sister LaToya published her own autobiography titled *LaToya: Growing Up in the Jackson Family*. Although LaToya would later assert that her then-husband, Jack Gordon, forced her to make many of the statements, at the time she wasn't hedging a thing. On the dust jacket she said: "Here is my book, the one my family doesn't want you to read."

Inside, she claimed that her father was a deeply disturbed and violent man. As a corollary, of course, she stated how compliant her mother Katherine was with her husband's reign of terror. LaToya described Joseph as a deranged patriarch with a maniacal will for his offspring to succeed — a monster around hearth and home as he drove his children to the top in the wider world.

The Jackson family is an all-in-one deal, according to LaToya. You get the American Dream and the American Nightmare all in one package. They rise from relative poverty to untold riches in a matter of a few short years. They started out as a family where the father worked in a steel mill and the mother in a department store, a family of 11 living in a two-bedroom house in the rough and tumble industrial stronghold of Gary, Indiana. They catapulted themselves by dint of dedication and hard work to a newly-rich family ensconced in a mansion on several acres in Encino, California, an exclusive and wildly expensive upscale suburb of Los Angeles in the dreamy San Fernando Valley. They went from Rust Belt rut to Sun Belt summit in one huge leap.

But, as *Growing Up in the Jackson Family* claims, the family puts on a happy face for the public while privately they suffer. LaToya claimed that Joseph didn't merely preside over his family — he took them hostage. She believed that he competed with his sons and made certain that all of them feared him to the point of death.

All of this left Michael, the star son in the family, with a hard assignment to negotiate in life. His sister told tales of how Michael, among all the sons, would prove to be the most defiant to Joseph's iron rule. Articulate and brave, Michael would speak up when he felt his father was wrong. LaToya said this would lead to their dad chasing him around the house to give him a beating. She described the boys, in training and rehearsal to become the legendary Jackson 5, being literally whipped by their father if they missed a note or sang off-key.

Joseph himself had once aspired to become a musician, and although he was left to see his children achieve the fame he once dreamed of, he kept his original guitar under lock and key in a bedroom closet. The boys had been forbidden ever to touch that guitar while Joseph was out of the house. But, unable to resist the temptation, they started to sneak the guitar out of the closet while their dad was away at work and their mother looked the other way. Tito had a natural affinity for the guitar, playing it without instruction. Then one day, a string broke.

When Joe got home, the boys hoped to convince him that the guitar had simply popped a string in the closet. But Joe got to the bottom of things and whaled on the boys. Then he took Tito, crying from his beating, into a bedroom and challenged him to show what he could do with the instrument. That's when Joe saw the potential in Tito, and before you know it, he was rehearsing his five oldest sons in the living room nearly every night.

At the time Joseph Jackson started these all-out rehearsals on a daily basis, Michael was all of 5 years old. Yet, even at this stage, he was clearly the most talented Jackson. He had the best taste among the boys for what the group should wear while performing. Even as the youngest performing son in the Jackson 5, Michael had the biggest voice about what the group would play, how they would play it and what they would wear while playing it. His vote also dominated what choreography the boys would employ on stage.

In later years, Michael will repeatedly mourn the loss of his childhood, telling interviewers how he would hear other children his age at play while he rehearsed with his brothers and how jealous the sounds would make him. He would talk about being caged in the recording studios at Motown or in L.A. and watching through the windows as other children cavorted on nearby playgrounds. Still, at the time, he embraced and rose to the challenges.

When LaToya described her father presiding over her brothers, she says that all of the boys feared Joseph and did what they were told — except for Michael. He would defy his father, talking back and often had to run for his life, flying to his mother's side for protection or hiding under furniture.

Joseph continued to play with his amateur music group, the Falcons. He would travel for gigs to Chicago and all over northern Illinois and northern Indiana, making it a point to study what other groups were wearing, what they were playing, how they were moving on stage and how they arranged their music. He would share all of this with his sons once he returned home, incorporating these things into the act the boys were perfecting. Another thing Joe did was have his sons listen constantly to the radio, paying close attention to how all the big acts and big stars achieved their effects.

Soon Joe had the boys booked as warm-up acts for bigger stars and well-known groups working the hot clubs in Gary and even in Chicago. This is how Michael came to emulate stars like Sam Cooke, Jackie Wilson, Otis Redding, and James Brown, the Godfather of Soul, performing with his Fabulous Flames. To complement this exposure to music for his boys, Joe also let them sit in when he and his own brother, the boys' uncle, played '50s rock-and-roll standards in their rhythm and blues band, the Falcons. The Jackson 5 were entered into all of the amateur competitions Joseph could reach. He would take them as far afield as the clubs in Chicago and Detroit and to such venerated sites as the Uptown in Philly and, in their supreme amateur triumph, to victory on the hallowed stage at the Apollo in Harlem.

From all of these experiences and sources, the boys continued to learn to pattern their act after the leading groups of the era. They studied The Temptations, The Four Tops, Smokey Robinson and the Miracles, and Little Anthony and the Imperials. They saw the Supremes live and Gladys Knight and the Pips. From these highly disciplined acts the Jackson 5 cherry-picked elements that they would incorporate in their own stage act.

And here again Michael was the quickest study and the best judge, proving to be quicksilver fast at picking up any and all dance steps. Everyone marveled at the way he could watch a routine once and replicate all of the choreography with the accuracy of an echo.

———

Joseph Jackson's drive came from a personal background filled with struggle. He had been born in Arkansas and brought up poor in Tennessee, where his father was an underpaid schoolteacher who took no nonsense from his students or from his own children. Joe's father, the Jackson children's grandfather, was a Lutheran with a vengeance, both strict and harsh in meting out discipline.

Later in life, Joseph would come to identify with his aggressor father and thanked him for instilling such discipline. Joseph felt that without his father's rigid inculcation of discipline, he would not have been able to accomplish in life what he was able, by dint of hard work and dedication, to do. This included, of course, creating and training the Jackson 5.

There is ample evidence as well that mother Katherine did not rein her husband in when he resorted to corporal punishment. LaToya stated that sometimes, after Joseph had punished one of his sons, leaving the boy a crying on the living room floor, Katherine would come into the room when the storm had passed and say quietly, "It's not worth it, Joe." Still, in general she employed her husband's patriarchal strength and his physical prowess to enforce her will. Katherine played the controlling and willful queen to Joseph's angry and vengeful king.

So here is the Jackson family on the climb to greatness — held hostage by their father's ambition. According to LaToya's book, Joe was overdetermined and brutal. He was also a gun nut, and in his rages, he has been known to brandish weapons. His temper reportedly terrified visiting neighborhood children. According to sources, he grabbed a knife on one occasion and threatened to use it. But he, above all else, was fixated on success and didn't seem to care a wit for the price paid by his children to attain it.

In the family dynamic, LaToya wrote that, Joe was savage and brutal with physical beatings for all of his sons. She claimed he especially picked on oldest son

Jackie, and he verbally bullied brilliant younger son, Michael, destined in less than two decades to be the world's greatest entertainer.

Mother Katherine was religious and attended Kingdom Hall as a devout Jehovah's Witness on a regular basis. Her children accompanied her, two of them becoming as devoted to the faith as their mother. The two are second daughter LaToya and fifth son Michael, who, separated in age by only a few years, are the closest of siblings. Michael and his sister accompanied their mother on missionary work for their faith, knocking on doors and visiting families in an effort to spread their faith.

The Jehovah's Witnesses, ironically, abhor singing, dancing, drinking, smoking, cursing and any sexual activity outside the sacred union of marriage. All day Sunday and through much of the week, Michael accompanied his mother to Kingdom Hall to pray and then traveled to the doorsteps and porches of strangers to preach conversion. Yet during the week, he rehearsed with his brothers as a member of the Jackson 5 in preparation for a career in showbiz.

On many nights, the fledgling Jackson 5 performed in risque and often funky, if not out-and-out raunchy, clubs and honkytonks, principally in Gary, nicknamed "Sin City," and in Chicago, known internationally for the fervor and wildness of its nightlife.

The oldest member of the group, Jackie, was still only in his early teens. On a regular basis, Michael, before he reached double digits in age, witnessed strippers peel down to full nudity and flip their discarded panties and G-strings to hooting men, high or inebriated, in the audience, who shouted lewd remarks. On a memorable night that Michael has described on numerous occasions, he, as a very young child, witnessed a beautiful stripper get down to the buff only to reveal that she was a he.

Later, when the Jackson 5 were famous and on tour, Michael pretended to sleep while his older brothers romped with groupies in the same hotel rooms and suites. According to numerous sources, father Joseph sometimes snuck groupies past hotel security.

All of the boys felt bad for their mother, waiting at home devoutly and religiously while their father, who never attended church or set foot in Kingdom Hall, lived the life of a libertine. Katherine, though beautiful, was, as previously mentioned, scarred as a child by a bout with polio that left her with a permanent limp and felt obligated to Joseph for taking a romantic interest in her and marrying her.

In later years, many reports claimed that Joe openly took on a succession of mistresses, and that he even fathered a daughter by one of these women, embarrassing the entire Jackson family and humiliating Katherine. LaToya noted in her autobiography that all of the Jackson children tended to marry young in an effort to free themselves from the parental home, where both Joe and Katherine tried to keep them in residence for as long as possible. This retention of their children at home is in keeping with the fortress mentality the Jackson parents fostered, the us-against-the-world mentality they instilled in all of their children.

As his brothers try to break away from this

semi-imprisonment with their parents in Hayvenhurst, the family mansion in Encino, Michael stays put. He continued to live there well into his '20s, when most young men would want their own apartment or home, especially a young man with the resources of Michael Jackson, by this time internationally famous and rich beyond imagination. Sister LaToya also remained at home. Like Michael, she remained at Hayvenhurst well into her 20s, and the two in fact had bedrooms across the hall from each other.

Later, LaToya claimed that she witnessed bizarre behavior at Hayvenhurst on Michael's part. She wasn't alone in lodging such allegations. Security personnel also asserted in an affidavit that they knew of many instances where Michael would sneak young boys into his bedroom right under the noses of his parents.

Michael's sister also disclosed in interviews to other strange behavior — her brother kept a human brain in a jar in his bedroom in the family home. Even more bizarre, she once claimed that he kept soiled diapers. If true, does this indicate a penchant on Michael's part for pedophilia compounded by coprophilia, an obsessive interest in feces?

Both Michael and LaToya appeared during this time period to vie too enthusiastically for Katherine's approval. They bonded with her against their father while attending services at Kingdom Hall and accompanied her on proselytizing trips to knock on the doors of strangers. Michael was, by this time, famous beyond belief, so he wore disguises when making these missionary housecalls. He later said that he loved to visit normal houses and see normal people going about their normal business. He liked to see houses with shag rugs and Barcaloungers and La-Z-Boys and people watching TV in their slippers. On these visits, he maintained that his disguises would always fool the parents, but never the children, who invariably recognized him right off the bat. He cited this as an instance of why he prefers the company of children, describing their superior intelligence, bold honesty and ineradicable innocence.

It is interesting to note that LaToya claimed during these years that she was completely innocent of sexual knowledge and a virgin. If true, this abstention from sex could be interpreted as a bid on her part to appease her mother and win her affection and approval as a model Jehovah's Witness, living completely within the puritanical strictures of that religious denomination. In a similar vein, Michael seemed to form a silent compact with his mother that she will never be replaced when it comes to love. No girlfriend or wife threatens mother Katherine's primary place in Michael's affections. This is an arrangement, subconscious and never formalized, made with their mothers by many gay men. Recently, in the New York Review of Books, Gary Wills pointed out that just such an arrangement is apparently common, though always unstated, between gay Catholic clergyman and their mothers.

Of course there are contradictions here. LaToya later claimed in interviews that her father sexually molested her. If these allegations are true, she may have remained technically virgins but hardly unknowledgeable about certain sexual activity. In the same way, it would be difficult to believe that Michael could be asexual during these years if he was, as his bodyguards later alleged in a court affidavit, seen sneaking young boys into his bedroom. When pedophilia charges were filed in court in 1993 against Michael, LaToya claimed in interviews that mother Katherine said that the family had to face the fact that Michael was "a faggot."

Whatever the truth of the Jackson family domestic scene may be, there is ample evidence that LaToya is the brave child who has broken the family code of silence. For confirmation of this sad state of affairs, you only have to read the dedication in her autobiography, *LaToya: Growing Up in the Jackson Family.* In it, she stated: "I dedicate this book to all the children of the world and to people who have suffered any form of abuse, in the hope that one day everyone will see the light and the abuse will end."

As you read about Michael Jackson, never lose sight of this fact: If his downfall is a tragedy, and it bears all of the classical hallmarks of a tragedy, then he is that saddest of all victims.

Abuse is cyclical. Biographer Christopher Andersen claims that Joseph and Katherine Jackson were themselves abused children, brought up rough and poor, with too many rules and too little affection, at the tail end of the Great Depression. The universal blind spot for abusive parents is that they are incapable of seeing themselves as anything but well intentioned. They believe that, through showing nothing but harshness to their children, they are preparing them well for the psychological, emotional and economic battering that adult life can hand out so freely. But in so doing they deny and abort a stage of human development where love and nurturing and affection and support have to be given freely in order, ironically, to prepare any child to cope later on with the harsh realities of adult life.

According to experts, abused children go through life feeling incomplete. They feel something essential has been taken from them. They feel robbed of a true childhood. This crippling emotional fate then swings wide the door to self-destructive and addictive behavior.

"No one is going to catch me, lady, and make me a man. I want always to be a little boy and to have fun." — Peter to Mrs. Darling in Peter Pan, Act Five.

CHAPTER 3

Michael Jackson, like Peter Pan looking for his shadow, has searched all of his life for that magic something that will complete him. He has looked in vain for that elusive element that will make him feel at home with himself. He has turned himself upside down and inside out to find the missing ingredient that will make him feel fulfilled.

Jackson has said on many occasions that he is not overly interested in material things, in the possessions that his great wealth once brought. There is no reason not to believe him. But, equally, there is every reason to believe that his search for self-satisfaction will be a losing venture as long as he concentrates on externals.

The message Michael got from his parents was that he wasn't enough. Joe Jackson was a driven perfectionist, a man obsessed with his sons' achieving perfection to the point where he seemed deranged by it. It is as if he lived vicariously through his sons and pushed them to greatness.

Then, when they achieved the greatness he pushed

them to, it appears that Joe Jackson turned around and resented his talented sons for usurping and surpassing him.

LaToya said Joe's wife Katherine may have done the same thing, only in different and more subtle and controlling ways. She may well have been more injurious to her children than husband Joe. Hers was the subtle poison of possessiveness, psychological and emotional. Her children were everything to her. To lose control of them would be shattering.

As an adult, probably through fate and through no fault of her own, Katherine had achieved nothing in the world except working briefly as a salesclerk for Sears. Anyone who has ever worked as a salesclerk in a middlebrow, chain department store knows how unfulfilling that is. Dealing with the public in low-end retailing is a draining job. Picture Katherine bearing nine children, working as a clerk in Sears, coming home bone weary but overjoyed to see her children and knowing that, through her efforts and sacrifice, they would have a better chance in life than she has had. Yet she needs and wants to own them as her proudest creations and her crowning achievements.

Daughter LaToya, the outspoken child of the Jackson family, told of her mother's machinations to keep her as a constant companion long after she is a full-grown woman. Katherine lost her oldest daughter Rebbie to an early marriage. So she was doubly determined to retain LaToya. When LaToya met husband-to-be Jack Gordon, mother Katherine set to work to prevent the budding relationship. Of course, in Katherine's defense, Gordon was a shady Las Vegas character.

Still, according to LaToya, Katherine tried almost everything to keep her daughter from Jack Gordon's side, going so far as to try to engineer a professional kidnapping of her one night in Manhattan at the Jockey Club on Central Park South. LaToya also claimed that her mother planted a bodyguard at her side whose job it was to be an inside informer, supposed to betray her movements and make it possible to snatch her back to the family bosom via what private eyes and security people call a "professional extraction."

Like everything one reads about the Jackson family, this alleged kidnapping attempt and the planting of a provocateur bodyguard is a bizarre story. If the stories are true, the dysfunction of the Jacksons as a family overwhelm even the show business competition, which is steep. They make the Osbournes of MTV fame look like the highly cosmeticized Nelsons of Ozzie and Harriet.

In mid autumn of 2002, a matter of a few weeks after Michael entertained visiting publishers, Jack Gordon visited New York City literary agents and pitched his inside account of life with the Jackson family. Although he and LaToya are now divorced, Gordon still had much to say. He went so far as to allege that Katherine had ordered mob-like rubouts of her enemies and of people who had displeased her. This allegation is even more extreme, and possibly more wildly paranoid, than LaToya's own repeated fears of her mother's wrath, stated by her over the years in her autobiography and in newspaper and magazine interviews.

LaToya constantly asserted that she believed her mother would have her snatched away and returned to the family compound at Hayvenhurst, to be held there as a virtual prisoner. She hinted broadly that her mother would go to any lengths to get her way, adding that her family was inordinately powerful and that they would stop at nothing to get what they wanted and to protect their interests.

Ozzy Osbourne, the head of his household, spewing obscenities and biting the heads off chickens and bats, is a humanitarian geek next to the kind of allegations Jack Gordon makes about matriarch Katherine Jackson. According to Jack Gordon, Joe Jackson was a creampuff when measured against his juggernaut of a wife.

But none of the Jacksons has been walloped in the media over the last decade more than megastar Michael. The reason? Michael Jackson has implicated himself in breaking — or has possibly even broken — the most sacred covenant of American society.

No entertainer before Michael Jackson ever seemed more dedicated to children, not even Walt Disney himself. Michael's largesse to children is indisputable. He has helped thousands of children around the world and been instrumental in getting them food, shelter and clothing, saving countless lives with his generosity. His philanthropic work where children are concerned is beyond question.

Yet, ironically, children have been his downfall.

The allegations of sexual child abuse against him have not led to conviction, much less a prosecution, in a court of law. But in the court of public opinion, Michael Jackson has been found wanting where the sexual welfare of children comes into the picture.

Michael has associated himself with a series of handsome male child stars and he has shed them serially as the boys aged, appearing to trade down for a younger version time after time. These young boys Michael befriends are like Alfie, the discarded lover boy and gigolo played so superbly by Michael Caine in the 1966 classic film of the same name. Caine ages and ends up out in the cold. At the end of the film, he has a last confrontation with Shelley Winters, once a steady client for his sexual favors. She is sprawled on silk sheets in a king size bed with a very young man. Standing in the bedroom doorway, Caine asks, "What's he got that I haven't got?"

The answer? "He's younger," Winters says.

Michael Jackson is reported to have admitted to one British boy, once the object of obsession, that he was no longer interested in the lad now that he was older. The boy was all of 17 or so when a source says Michael effectively told him his shelf life had expired.

———

As Michael Jackson continually searched for happiness in the faces of youth, his own appearance began to change through plastic surgery. He will ultimately undergo what some have estimated to be seven nose jobs. Photos now show that Michael's nose is collapsing, held in place by rubber implants. There are other reports that these implants are so prominent now that Michael practically dons his nose each morning the way other people brush their teeth or comb their hair or put on lipstick or a pair of eyeglasses.

Michael Jackson for years has undergone other forms of plastic surgery. During Michael's teen years, he suffered terrible bouts with acne. This gave father Joe another verbal lever with which to pull the switch on his genius of a son and attack his young ego. According to both Taraborrelli and Andersen, Joseph mocked Michael's pimples and his pitted skin. The result? Years later Michael is said to have undergone numerous skin peels at the hands of plastic surgeons in attempts to remove permanent facial scars left by the acne.

If only Michael Jackson stopped there with remaking his image. Professional plastic surgeons looking at before-and-after pictures of Michael state their personal opinion that among other things:

■ He has clearly had cheek implants.

■ That he has had a cleft put in his chin.

■ That he has had his eyebrows raised and permanent eyeliner placed on his eyelids.

■ That he has had crow's feet removed and his cheeks tightened and his chin tucked.

In addition, for years a controversy has raged over whether or not Michael Jackson bleaches his skin in an attempt to lighten it. Michael himself testified that he did not do this. He told Oprah Winfrey on her show in 1993 that he was not trying to lighten his skin. He said instead that he suffered from a skin disease called vitiligo. Vitiligo causes the skin to lighten dramatically in patches, disfiguring its victims with splotchy complexions. Michael claimed that he took lightening agents for his skin so that he would not look hideously disfigured by vitiligo.

Sister LaToya, however, discounted Michael's explanation years ago. She pointed out that there was no history in the large Jackson family of any such skin disease, and she expressed her belief that Michael wanted to be white. She also pointed out that for years while she and Michael were still in residence in Hayvenhurst, Michael would have a cavalcade of young boys brought to the house. He would spend days and nights sequestered in his bedroom with these young visitors, referred to as his "special friends." She said at the time that they were always Caucasian boys, often blond and blue-eyed. That would mean that Michael's only special relationship with an African-American boy was with Emmanuel Lewis, child TV star of the hit show Webster, back in the early '80s.

Michael's preference was clearly for these "special" boys to be white. This would seem to tie in with Michael's quest to lighten his skin. Several observers have pointed out that Michael's skin at times has been an unnatural white, a whiter-than-white kind of albino whiteness.

Then, just last fall, when Jack Gordon was making the rounds in New York City pitching his book on the Jackson family to literary agents, he said that Michael used chemicals to bleach his skin white. Gordon claimed that this had nothing to do with any disease.

According to Jack Gordon, Michael did not use these bleaching agents on his genitals, and he claimed that this was a key point in verifying the testimony of the young boy, Jordan Chandler, whose reported allegations of sexual misconduct had brought Michael's alleged pedophilia into the public eye.

If the descriptions of Michael Jackson's genitals were given in court-registered depositions by Jordan Chandler, Michael Jackson would eventually have to submit to court-ordered photography of his genitals. According to Jack Gordon, the unbleached and original dark pigmentation of Michael's genitals was the key to corroborating the young boy's testimony. But there are also other reports that Michael had a tattoo on or near his genitals of none other than Winnie the Pooh. But the existence of this tattoo has never been confirmed. A weeping Michael in a famous TV address on CNN would later describe the photography of his private parts as the most humiliating moment of his life. Considering the barbaric treatment he allegedly suffered at the hands of his father, that is saying a lot.

———

Michael's attempts to alter his looks and the suggestion that he changed his skin color have alienated many black people, as they should. Michael Jackson started life as a really handsome kid with a winning smile and a beautiful face. He has abused plastic surgery to the degree that he is now, in terms of looks, a freak. He has made himself look half feminine and half masculine. He looks perfectly androgynous.

His attempts to give himself the features and complexion of a white person are repulsive to black people wise and old enough to remember a time when the looks and features of black people were vilified and denigrated. It was not until the "Black Is Beautiful" movement of the '60s that this dreadful and inhumane and simply stupid social branding was arrested and eventually reversed. As long as 15 years ago, Don King spoke out against the wholesale alterations to his looks Michael Jackson was subjecting himself to.

King had produced the Jacksons' Victory tour not long before he stated in the press: "I've got to talk to Michael Jackson. Blacks are not happy with what he's doing to himself. Michael cannot become white, no matter how many nips and cuts he gets." King added, "He is trying to totally disassociate himself from blacks... Blacks see this as an attempt for him to become less black." To many people, there seems no question that sister LaToya and people like Don King are right about Michael's overdone plastic surgery and his overdetermined bleaching of his complexion.

But what is more important is this: Almost all of what is considered Michael's trademark bizarre behavior is indicative of a deep-seated dissatisfaction with himself. He seems to loathe himself, to see himself always as incomplete, imperfect, unsatisfactory and unworthy. All of this pathology could be traced back to parental or cultural abuse, however indirect, however unintentional.

Michael Jackson biographers like J. Randy Taraborrelli and Christopher Andersen have theorized that Michael couldn't tolerate or live with his original looks because they were too similar to his hated father's. That seems plausible but hardly the whole reason. After all, Michael's brother Jermaine has testified in the press that he was frightened of his father and that his father often taunted him as "ugly," just the way he did with Michael.

Yet neither Jermaine nor any of the other three brothers has altered his looks dramatically through surgery, and certainly none has tried to lighten the color of his skin.

Michael, of course, as theorized earlier, was the son who got into the unwinnable Oedipal warfare with his father most severely. He was the defiant one. He was the one LaToya said was most often beaten. Yet he was also the one his father could not do without in terms of realizing his family dreams in show business. Joe was no fool when it came to musical and singing talent, and he knew Michael was the star of the Jackson show right from the time Michael was only 5 years old.

You can see this quest for the missing something acting in reverse with Michael as well. That is, you see him looking for substitute parents, especially a substitute mother. For years he is pampered and mothered by Diana Ross. This leads to hero worship on Michael's part taken to the depths of pathology. His first experiences under the plastic surgeon's scalpel are designed to make him look like a male version of idol and surrogate mother figure Diana

Ross. Michael states openly that he wants to look like Diana.

Later Michael moves on from identification with Diana Ross as a surrogate mother to the same type of identifications with female luminaries like Kate Hepburn, Liza Minnelli and, more than with any other woman, Elizabeth Taylor. Michael's identification with Liz becomes obsessive.

Michael's real mother Katherine becomes explosively and publicly angry with her son when, in the fullness of the alleged pedophilia crisis, she is barred from seeing him while Liz Taylor has round-the-clock access to Michael. In fact, Liz took total control of Michael and his well-being at the apex of the 1993 pedophilia accusations and media frenzy.

But the fact remains, stark and raw: It appears that Michael Jackson has expended a lot of energy in search of a surrogate mother. Perhaps, as others suggest, he did not get the proper parenting from his biological parents. Were father Joe and mother Katherine emotionally, intellectually, or psychologically equipped to properly nurture a talented, intelligent and gifted boy on Michael Jackson's level?

What about surrogate fathers? Michael seems to have surrounded himself with powerful advisers, bodyguards, managers, voice coaches, musicians, arrangers, lawyers, doctors, and music and entertainment industry executives. But he does not seem to have related to them as paternal surrogates. He did not cede control of his life to them. It's almost as if one father was quite enough for Michael Jackson.

He doesn't seem to need another domineering male to take over his life. He famously fired his father Joe as his manager when his success outside the family group, The Jacksons, dictated such a break.

This had to be quite a boon for Michael, in terms of sweet revenge. Giving the heave-ho to an oppressor is always satisfying, especially so if the oppressor in question is your father.

———

Michael Jackson is reputed to be a business wizard in creative areas, though a disaster at handling his business and personal finances. He could earn prodigious sums of money, but he was not good at managing it. He squandered his savings foolishly and mismanaged it fairly openly.

With money, Michael was notoriously impulsive. He apparently thought nothing of dropping into a toy store after official hours with one of his special relationship boys and slapping thousands of dollars in purchases onto his credit cards. He spent fortunes on security personnel and security systems. His art collection is stunningly expensive, featuring the works of classical and modern masters, much of it bought at expensive auction houses in London, New York, Los Angeles and Paris. He built a private zoo stocked with 200 animals, many of them exotic and highly expensive both to purchase and maintain, and he built a mind-boggling private amusement park at his 2,700-acre ranch in the Santa Ynez Valley. Around the world, he bought expensive residences, including a penthouse suite in Trump Tower in Manhattan and a castle in France.

With his "special relationship" boys he would trot around the globe, sequestering them in wildly expensive suites at the world's most exclusive and deluxe hotels and resorts. Millions came in and millions went out.

So, as Michael Jackson held court for visiting publishers in the Westin Hotel in Stamford, Connecticut, in reduced circumstances, he was one day short of his 44th birthday. He had gone from the world's most famous, recognizable and popular entertainer to a man largely mocked and notorious, rather than famous, and either reviled or pitied by most of his former millions of fans. He had gone from a man earning staggering sums of money annually to a man who had mostly gone through a personal net worth of a quarter billion dollars. His earning prospects today were a mere shadow of what they'd been nine years earlier.

This is not surprising, since he has a nut estimated as high as $20 million annually to maintain his lifestyle. Some reports claim he is heavily in debt and staving off bankruptcy by a skin-of-his-teeth margin. His latest record album has bombed so publicly that he has resorted to having the Reverend Al Sharpton assail Sony Music kingpin Tommy Mottola. Sharpton inveighed against Mottola and Sony for what were widely perceived to be trumped up charges of racism that allegedly undermined Michael's sales. This is of course ludicrous. The notoriously crass music business puts money before any other consideration.

Certainly they did this when Michael's albums were selling from 20 to 40 million copies worldwide.

———————

Michael Jackson's sister LaToya has told the world that her brother Michael is captivated by his three favorite movies, Peter Pan, The Wizard of Oz and E.T. All three movies are about children or a childlike alien searching for love and identity and purpose and family connection. All three films are about the search for that magical something that renders one complete and satisfactory and comfortable within oneself.

But Michael Jackson failed to learn important lessons from these movies, especially from The Wizard of Oz. What Michael Jackson failed to learn is what the Wizard taught Dorothy and the Cowardly Lion and the Tin Man and the Scarecrow. What you mistakenly perceive as a lack within you is actually available to you as a plus within you, if only you'd wake up to your hidden potential and actualize it. Life is about realizing all that lies within you.

Michael Jackson has been on a lifelong search for happiness, for that magical something that will at once eradicate his disastrous and lost childhood and render him whole and at peace. That peace, according to Michael, was found only by spending time with children, who loved him just for himself.

"My boy will show the world he's a man — I know one day he will come home to face the music." — Katherine Jackson, on December 7, 1993.

CHAPTER 4

The crisis struck as Michael Jackson triumphantly breezed into Bangkok for the Asian launch of his Dangerous world tour. As usual, a large entourage accompanied him, including a small army of security personnel. They swept into Bangkok's luxe Oriental Hotel and Michael took his usual regal penthouse suite. Eight days before his 35th birthday, Michael was about to get the worst kind of publicity. Before his luggage could be unpacked, his criminal attorney, Howard Weitzman, was on the phone with urgent news. Earlier that day in America, not many hours after Michael and company had departed LAX for Thailand, police had raided both his Neverland Valley Ranch, as well as his lavish condo in L.A.'s posh Century City.

The posses of police officers and investigators were looking for possible evidence and conclusive proof that Michael Jackson, the earth's most famous, popular, and recognizable male, was a child molester. In both locations, the police had moved in swiftly, armed with search warrants. At the Neverland

Ranch, Michael's security forces had briefly attempted to turn the huge task force of policemen and investigators away, but once the police flashed their court ordered warrants under the noses of the guards, the security personnel stepped aside and stood helplessly by.

The police had not come unprepared. A lot of forethought had gone into their early morning raid. At the Neverland Ranch they brought a locksmith with them. Then they demanded that Michael's domestic staff give way as they opened the securely locked door the secret playroom, which Michael had declared off limits at all times to all but him and any of his special friends.

The Secret Playroom was small, only about 6 feet by 8 feet, and it was kept in darkness except for the light cast by a 30-inch Trinitron television set. There was only one piece of furniture in the entire room, an oversized sofa. Whenever a Neverland staffer got a brief glimpse of this room, usually while delivering food that Michael had ordered from the kitchen for him and his visitor, the special friend would be perched on the sofa, but always fully clothed when Michael opened the door.

For years Michael's protectors, apologists and flacks would subject what was now happening, these police raids and searches, to spin and counterspin moves. They would attempt to make out that Michael Jackson, as befitting a celebrity of unimaginable dimensions, was being victimized in extortion schemes by ruthless and greedy opportunists. He would be portrayed as the innocent and hapless lover of all children who was now being exploited in a dastardly fashion by despicable parents hell-bent on extracting a fortune from Michael's overflowing coffers on the spurious grounds that he had engaged in inappropriate sexual activity with their young son.

Who made the accusation that precipitated all of this? None other than the father of a 13-year-old boy with whom Michael Jackson had been seen with for the past six months. According to the boy's natural father — his son had confided in him that Michael Jackson had engaged in sexual acts with him. The father claimed that the boy told him that Michael had brought him to sexual climaxes both manually and orally. The boy was named Jordan Chandler, nicknamed Jordie. His father, Evan, was a Los Angeles dentist who had written a few screenplays and yearned to crack into the entertainment business.

Like the boy's mother, June, his dentist father had at first been flattered that his son had attracted the attention and affection of a megastar of Michael's proportions. The mother was remarried to Dave Schwartz, the man who started the highly lucrative Rent-A-Wreck business.

Mother June, a beautiful Oriental woman, son Jordie, and his younger sister, Lily, had been keeping company with Michael for about six months prior to the outbreak of the scandal. They had been written up in the press as Michael Jackson's secret family.

During the six months Michael was associated with Jordie and his mother and sister, he had lavished astonishing gifts on all of them. He had taken them to the Neverland Ranch almost every weekend. Sometimes he would phone the family as many as four times a day. He had taken them on trips to Las Vegas, to Disney World in Florida, to Monaco, and to Paris. He lavished $20,000 worth of jewelry on mom June, including a ruby bracelet, ring and earrings. He bought Jordie about $20,000 worth of computer equipment, and took him on sprees buying toys that carried tabs as high as $1,500. He also purchased toys for little sister Lily. When Michael took the family with him to Monte Carlo for the World Music Awards, he threw in a side trip to Euro Disney.

On the five-day excursion to Las Vegas, he had the three of them stay with him at his private three-bedroom villa at The Mirage Hotel. The first full day they spent in Vegas Michael took Jordie shopping and then to the hotel's arcade. But they couldn't stay at the arcade long because other children playing the video games started to crowd around Michael. But later that night Michael and Jordie swam in the hotel's dolphin pool with the dolphins. The next day they went shopping again and then Michael took Jordie and Lily to the "Siegfried and Roy" show. The next night, Michael and Jordie ate dinner at the Mirage's Chinese restaurant. Waiter Chad Jahn, who served their table, said, "They talked in whispers and laughed like a father and son."

Jordie's later lawsuit against the superstar reportedly claimed that because of these "expensive and lavish gifts," Michael "was able to seduce plaintiff and thereby defendant Michael Jackson was able to satisfy his lust, passions and sexual desires."

It later came to light that Michael induced Jordie to watch the movie The Exorcist while perched on Michael's bed with him. When Jordie became frightened while watching scary scenes in the movie, Michael is alleged to have cuddled with him to comfort the boy. Jordie Chandler's lawyer, Larry R. Feldman, was prepared to argue in court that this, on Michael's part, was part and parcel of an elaborate seduction scheme.

How did the scandal break? What happened was this: When Jordie Chandler spent time with his real father Evan, the dentist, under the terms of the joint custody arrangement between his parents, Michael Jackson came to the father's house to spend the night with Jordie. The father became suspicious of the sleeping arrangements his son had with the pop legend. Christopher Andersen says the father claims that he started to quiz his son about whether there was any physical contact between him and Michael. That's when Andersen claims the son obliquely started to indicate that there was.

A few days later, after extracting a tooth from Jordie, while the boy was still groggy from the anesthetic, Evan Chandler asked his son straight out if Michael Jackson had ever touched his penis. According to the dentist, Jordie said, low and soft and confessional, one word. "Yes."

This alleged admission galvanized Jordie's father to

take his son to be evaluated by Beverly Hills psychiatrist Dr. Mathis Abrams, with whom the father had consulted a short while earlier about the whole situation and whether it was healthy or not for his son. At that first consultation between Evan Chandler and Dr. Mathis, son Jordie was not present and his father did not reveal to Dr. Mathis that the man more than 20 years older than his son was indeed Michael Jackson.

Andersen says a meeting followed on August 4 in the penthouse suite of the Westwood Marquis Hotel in which Evan Chandler confronted Michael Jackson, with Michael's famous private eye friend and security consultant, Anthony Pellicano.

At this first showdown, Michael Jackson flatly denied that he had trespassed sexually on young Jordie Chandler. The father allegedly claimed he thought immediately from Michael's chilly smile and agitated body language that he was lying. According to Andersen, he asserted that he knew on the spot that Jackson had abused sexual boundaries with his son and that Jackson was in fact guilty of criminal behavior.

According to Andersen, the Jackson camp was convinced the father merely wanted to use the situation to boost his somewhat stalled career as a screenwriter.

So, two and a half weeks after this first meeting, Michael Jackson found himself in the penthouse suite in the Oriental Hotel in Bangkok fielding a phone call from his criminal lawyer, Howard Weitzman. Attorney Weitzman quickly informed his superstar client that both of his residences had been thoroughly searched earlier that day in California by a whole phalanx of police officers and investigators.

———

Michael Jackson was rocked to the core by this phone call from Weitzman. The thought that the police had invaded his privacy made him furious. His anxiety now sharply contrasted with the behavior Michael had exhibited two and a half weeks earlier after the showdown with Evan Chandler and his lawyer in the penthouse at the Westwood Marquis.

After that awkward confrontation, which Michael initially regarded as a bump in the road, he went back to living the way he had lived for 20 years or so. He went house-hunting with another special young friend, Brett Barnes, an Australian boy.

Michael and Brett really liked a French-style chateau in Beverly Hills that was gigantic and featured a built-in bowling alley and a dining room with a glass floor that looked down into an indoor swimming pool. The place also had an elevator and a marble ballroom.

In typical fashion, Michael and Brett ran from room to room, yukking it up the way kids do while exploring any new place. Michael was taking a very cavalier attitude to the storm brewing with the Chandlers. It was proving to be a storm that couldn't be diverted from its devastating path that would have it hit landfall right on top of Michael Jackson's head.

According to Andersen, Evan Chandler was not one to let grass grow beneath his feet. He wasn't about to play a waiting game with anyone on these serious issues, though Jackson insiders maintain to this day that Jordie's father wanted the $20 million to fund four movies to be based on four screenplays that Evan Chandler himself would write. The father counters these allegations with the flat statement that the money was to go into a trust fund for his son.

That's all moot now. Because Jordie's father took his son on the afternoon of August 17 to see Dr. Mathis Abrams while this dialogue was going back and forth between Jackson's people and attorney Larry R. Feldman, on behalf of the Chandlers.

Three hours after Jordie Chandler's session with Dr. Abrams, the psychiatrist picked up the phone and did what California law specified explicitly that he must do. He reported the child's allegation of sexual abuse by an adult to the Los Angeles County Department of Children's Services. A woman at that agency named Ann T. Rosato then interviewed Jordie.

That same day, Los Angeles Police Sergeant Tom Felix set in motion and headed up an official investigation. Sgt. Felix designated Officers E. Cateriano and J. Calams to interview Jordie as well. All of these authorities came to agree with Dr. Abrams that Jordie was telling the truth. And they were all shocked by the boy's story. They were bowled over by the lengths to which Michael Jackson appeared to have gone in order to influence this youngster.

For example, Michael Jackson had phoned several times every day for six months to talk to Jordie and he had laid on gifts, trips, toys and jewels.

The boom was about to be lowered on Michael Jackson.

———

"I imagine Michael Jackson is pretty scared right now — really scared. And he should be, because what he did to me is a really bad thing," Jordie Chandler said in an exclusive interview granted to the National Enquirer shortly after the story broke. "I'm just forgetting about the whole thing now. Michael hasn't called me or anything and I don't think he will."

From the mouths of babes, so to speak. The last thing that Michael Jackson was going to do is call Jordie Chandler. Michael was at least no longer in denial — the Jackson family hallmark reaction to life's unpleasant elements. No, he was in high scream and suffering from high anxiety. Back in the penthouse suite at the Oriental Hotel in Bangkok the psychodrama quickly escalated. The swift and decisive police action back in California had caught Michael's spin machine in a down cycle. The tables had quickly been turned on the Jackson camp.

And Michael came unglued. This was not unusual. Michael was given to jags of self-pity and to overly tearful reactions whenever he considered himself threatened. That is, he reverted to being the toddler cowering before his brutal and abusive father.

In the swank penthouse suite in Bangkok, no one could manage to comfort the Gloved One. He went into full meltdown and there was nothing anyone in his entourage could do to reverse his acting out. He screamed and threw things, running from room to room.

When criminal attorney Weitzman had first told Michael the news, he refused to accept it. The singer wanted to know how such a thing could happen to a person like him. He demanded to know how "they" could do such a thing, under what authority. Weitzman explained that the "they" in question, namely the police, had been empowered by the courts with search warrants. But this information inflamed rather than mollified Michael. He started to shout into the phone that everyone knew that he, Michael Jackson, was a benefactor of children. That he loved children. That he couldn't do enough for them.

When Michael had worked himself into a proper lather with Weitzman, he hurled the phone away from him and started on a rampage. He overturned furniture and threw and smashed a vase of flowers. He protested his innocence. His erratic behavior fits the pattern of someone guilty, most people would agree, and also that of someone who was in severe denial.

Compounding this situation, and aggravating it, was the fact that by this time Michael Jackson was noticeably — even obviously — hooked on pills. Ever since he had burned his scalp in a freak explosion and fire while filming one of his spectacular Pepsi commercials in 1984, he had been increasingly dependent on painkillers.

When the explosion occurred on stage at Los Angeles' Shrine Auditorium during the filming of the Pepsi commercial, Michael was saved from even more severe burns by the quick thinking of his bodyguard Miko Brando, Marlon's son. Miko Brando seriously burned his own hands in his courageous and successful attempts to put the fire out that had engulfed Michael's head and hair.

The cause of this accident was apparently a magnesium flash bomb that detonated a bit late. At any rate, the explosion burned Michael's nape and set his hair on fire, quite dramatically, with flames leaping upward. There were 3,000 fans in the auditorium at the time, watching Michael and his brothers perform for the commercial. They told reporters later that the smell of Michael's burning hair filled the large auditorium. Michael was rushed by ambulance to Cedars-Sinai Medical Center. He was put on painkillers and, apparently over the next nine years, he could not shake his dependence on them. He grew increasingly more reliant on the painkillers to get him through the day. So by the time the sexual molestation scandal broke in the summer of 1993, he was fully hooked.

———

Michael Jackson had become seriously out of control in his penthouse suite at the Oriental Hotel in Bangkok. But spin moves were progressing to get the superstar out of the possibly disastrous jam he had brought upon himself. One Jackson insider had this to say at the time regarding what it had been like during those first days sequestered in the hotel in Bangkok: "Michael was shattered. He wouldn't eat and he wouldn't talk. He just wanted to be alone. Michael isn't mad, he's hurt. He feels that he was very good to the people involved. They weren't strangers, they shared their lives. Michael is very childlike. He just can't understand why."

This account is only partially accurate. It has good spin but it's just another curveball. In reality, Michael was scaring all of those around him. He was wandering around the suite repeating himself and angry, unable to sleep. He simply passed out from time to time when the painkillers took him under. He sobbed uncontrollably on the bed for hours in bouts of spasms that shook his whole body. He cried. He was inconsolable. He was so stressed out that he started to mix drugs, adding tranquilizers to the mix of painkillers, further numbing himself to reality.

KNBC in Los Angeles broke the story on Monday, August 25, that police had raided both Michael Jackson's Neverland Ranch and his condo in Century City.

Still, no word of what lay behind the police raids would have broke had Jackson's camp not seized the initiative. Michael's spokesman on this issue, Anthony Pellicano, spoke before television cameras only hours before KNBC aired its story on the evening news. Billing himself as Michael Jackson's consultant on security, Pellicano stepped before the TV floodlights and announced that there was no truth to the charges that Michael Jackson had sexually molested or in any way abused a young boy. Pellicano downplayed the complicated matter as yet another instance of extortion being attempted on a grand scale with a megacelebrity worth multimillions. He characterized it as, more or less, same old, same old. He said that there were routinely 25 to 30 such attempts made on an annual basis to relieve Michael Jackson of some of his hard-earned wealth.

Pellicano told the reporters gathered for the news conference that Michael Jackson had been presented with a demand for $20 million. He said that neither Michael Jackson nor any of his advisers had any intention of taking this demand seriously. He said that the person making the demand had threatened to take his story to the district attorney. Pellicano cavalierly stated that he had invited this complainant to do just that.

When Michael Jackson and his advisers refused to pay any money, Pellicano said that the complainant made a call to the City of Los Angeles Department of Child and Family Services. That, Pellicano stated, was what started this whole investigation. That was why a dozen police cars carrying some 40 L.A. cops had arrived at Michael's ranch in Santa Ynez, California, and that was why another contingent of L.A. police showed up with a separate set of search warrants for Michael's ultra-expensive condo in Century City.

Until Pellicano opened his mouth to overwhelm the Chandlers with his counteroffensive, portraying them as golddigging blackmailers, no one knew why the police had carried out their early morning raids on Michael's two residences. Now the whole world knew. And the international press was quick to publish the allegations of child sexual abuse across the globe. Even the stately London Times trumpeted the allegations against Michael Jackson in a huge front-page headline.

Pellicano had played into the hands of the media, who are always starved for news stories in the dog days of late summer, the height of vacation season, when most governments around the world are also usually in recess. Michael Jackson thus got top billing for a story that was his worst nightmare. Many of the more sensational newspapers around the world wondered aloud in gigantic print whether Michael Jackson was a Pied Piper, a Peter Pan, or just another pervert. Some court watchers say Anthony Pellicano had made a serious mistake in handling the media. They argue that this was his second serious mistake because he had already underestimated the intelligence of the Chandler's lawyer, Larry R. Feldman. Jordie's dad Evan struck back with a vengeance at the implications that he was a blackmailer and an extortion artist instead of an outraged and morally offended parent.

When Pellicano left Michael to stew in his misery in Bangkok, he had told the world's most popular entertainer not to worry. Pellicano would cut the rope and lead Michael down from the scaffold the Chandler's had built to hang him from. Now, it seemed he had personally tightened the noose.

In the end, the state refused to prosecute, but it would cost Michael Jackson many millions of dollars to settle his civil suit with the Chandlers out of court.

The emotional costs to Michael Jackson, and the long-range ancillary costs were even higher.

———

Back at the penthouse suite in the Oriental Hotel in Bangkok, Michael Jackson was not holding up well at all. In a flash of his old bravado, he did pull himself together long enough to telephone Brett Barnes back in the States. Brett was staying at the Neverland Ranch. Michael assured his new young special friend that the whole police raid was a misunderstanding. It was just a case of people jumping to the wrong conclusions and making a really big mistake. Everything would be fine and everything would go back to normal. They would have lots of fun together as soon as this thing got cleared up. Brett was not to worry. He was to play with the toys and take rides in the amusement park until Michael could join him again.

That was about the only thing Michael pulled himself together enough to do. He canceled his second show in Bangkok only a few hours before he was slated to blast his way onto the stage. His tour doctor said, by way of explanation for the cancellation, that Michael was negatively affected by the heat and humidity in Bangkok. He said that Michael was dehydrated. This was nonsense. Bangkok was in fact cooler than usual for that time of year. Besides, the interior of the stadium where Michael was to perform was climate controlled. Still, Michael's public relations spokesman told reporters in Michael's penthouse suite that the superstar had lost too many fluids during the first performance in Bangkok the night before and that he was too exhausted to go on stage again so soon.

The truth was that Michael was wandering around his bedroom like a ghost of his former self. He was whacked out on Valium and Percodan, mixing the tranquilizer with the painkiller in a heady pharmaceutical cocktail. He was spotted by a hotel maid in his bed crouched in a fetal curl and sucking his thumb even as his mother Katherine tried frantically to get through to him on the phone. He had by this time so many sycophants and flunkies in his entourage that it was hard for anyone, even Michael's mother Katherine, to get through to him.

Finally, Michael called his mother after the story broke in the international press, thanks to Anthony Pellicano's televised press conference back in the City of Angels. Michael cried over the international lines to his mother. She reassured him that she knew he was innocent. This was a pretty bizarre comment for his mother to make in light of later allegations by Michael's sister LaToya that Michael's mother knew of the visits by young boys to Michael's room when she and Michael still lived at the family compound in Encino.

Michael told his mother tearfully over the phone that he couldn't possibly be arrested when he returned to the United States or he would have to kill himself.

This was not the first time over the course of the last few days in Bangkok that Michael had mentioned suicide as a possible way out of the mess that had developed around his life. Bill Bray was present in Michael's suite in Bangkok. He was familiar as the head of Jackson family security since the early days of the Jackson 5. He was an older man and a retired police officer. For Michael, he was a surrogate father of sorts, as well. Bray was not taking Michael's threats as idle chitchat. He ordered a suicide watch placed on Michael around the clock. The Gloved One was not to be left alone — someone in the vast security detail was to keep a lynx's eye on him at all times.

The seriousness of Michael's mental condition was confirmed for Bill Bray when Michael placed a call to the person he considered his closest friend in the entire world. He placed this call on August 25, the exact same day as Pellicano's press conference back in Los Angeles. He called a person as traumatized by child stardom as he himself was. He called a person as simultaneously addicted to, and repelled by, fame as he was. He called the star of National Velvet, Cat on a Hot Tin Roof, Butterfield 8, Cleopatra, and Who's Afraid of Virginia Woolf — Liz Taylor.

No one was, or could ever be, as close to a surrogate mother for him as Liz Taylor. She told him she believed him unconditionally when he said he was being persecuted and that he was innocent. She begged him not to harm himself. She implored him to be strong. She exhorted him to hold on.

Because, in the role of Fairy God Mother and Maternal Savior, Liz announced to Michael that she was on her way to Bangkok.

She would be at his bedside shortly.

Liz had been there for troubled geniuses before. She had smothered Montgomery "Monty" Clift and Rock Hudson in her amble bosom with maternal love in crisis after crisis.

And she would be there for the Gloved One.

"Thank God for Elizabeth Taylor. She protected me." — Michael Jackson, September 6, 1994.

CHAPTER 5

The spinmeisters around Michael Jackson went to work. They put out stories that the superstar was not affected by the accusations and allegations of child sexual abuse that had been lodged against him. Even though two concerts had been canceled in Bangkok because Michael was reported to be sick from dehydration, the public relations machine roared away on Michael's behalf. Pellicano had gone on the offensive back in L.A., and things looked promising.

African-American leaders like the Reverend Jesse Jackson had urged the media to use restraint until Michael Jackson could clear his name. Many entertainment industry stars, in addition, made statements supporting Michael. Obviously Pellicano's statement at his press conference that Michael received 25 to 30 extortion attempts a year was working to some extent.

Surprisingly, not one media person challenged Pellicano's statement. No one asked to see proof that Michael Jackson received extortion attempts and received them in that great a number.

Back in Asia, as this scandal was drawing headlines around the world, Micheal Jackson was anything but calm and untouched by it. The opposite was true. He had stopped eating and was suffering bouts of dizziness. He was also continuing to cry uncontrollably and to question how such a thing could happen to him.

Still, the tour moved on. Michael issued an official statement through his public relations armature that he would continue. He closed the statement to his fans by adding that he loved them all. This was a signature statement he made all of the time on stage at the conclusion of his concerts. As a high priest of pop culture touting love and tolerance as the keys to saving the world, Michael could do nothing less than maintain at this time of crisis that his message of universal love and tolerance applied more now than ever. He and his entourage moved on to the world-renowned Raffles Hotel in Singapore. They took over the entire third floor and Michael again retreated to his bedroom and total isolation. For he knew that help was on the way.

Back at LAX, Elizabeth Taylor had remained as good as her word. She had recently suffered a bad bout with pneumonia, and her health was not the best, yet she defied her doctor's advice and booked the first flight out to Singapore. She and her husband Larry Fortensky settled in for the arduous, 20-plus hour flight to the Far East dressed in sweats, Liz all in pink and Larry decked out all in white.

"Michael is more than my good friend," she

told reporters traveling with her on the flight. "He's family."

Liz flatly asserted that no one could love children more than Michael did. She characterized him as a man of outstanding integrity, a spiritual man and a religious man. She expressed confidence Michael would be found innocent of these charges and his good name exonerated. She asked that people show compassion for an artist as sensitive, kind and caring as Michael at such a trying time. She cited his abundant charitable work on behalf of children the world over. She even went so far as to put her imprimatur on Anthony Pellicano's bold spin move at his pressconference a few days earlier. She stated that it was obvious to her that what lay behind this whole debacle and sideshow was an attempt at extortion.

———————

When Liz and Larry arrived in Singapore in the early morning hours on August 29, they went straight to the hotel and checked in. Then Liz went directly to Michael's room.

When Michael opened the door, the two embraced and Liz reassured him that things would work out. She knew of the fears his staff had for his health and his life, and she could plainly see the toll this whole ordeal was taking on him. He had lost weight, he was sobbing and he seemed stunned, dazed and out of it.

Even before Liz arrived, some of Michael's advisers had urged him to cancel the rest of his tour.

They wanted him to undergo a complete physical. But Michael wanted to press on. He insisted that he could not let his fans down. He was being unrealistic. His vomiting had increased in intensity and frequency, according to reports, and he was complaining of ferocious headaches. Both these symptoms can be manifestations of acute anxiety.

Michael had pulled himself together in anticipation of Liz's visit, decorating her suite extensively with orchids. He also purchased a stuffed toy tiger and had it placed on her bed with a note that declared his love for her and Larry. After all, Michael had famously hosted the couple's lavish wedding a few years earlier at his Neverland Ranch.

One staff member at Neverland, however, would later disclose to the media that Liz and Michael's intimate relationship was hyped as a kind of camouflage. This staffer claimed that Liz would come to the ranch for extended visits and Michael would hardly see her at all, especially when he had one of his special little friends in attendance. Michael would stay in his suite of rooms with one of his special friends, including the off-limits-to-all Secret Playroom that was always locked and in which Michael was never to be disturbed for any reason. Liz would be isolated in the guest quarters, where the staffer said that she would almost invariably dine alone.

Michael and Liz had a history of sharing medical problems. A while back when Michael was in the midst of an enthusiasm for herbal therapy, he had Liz see his herbalist and she later said that she felt cured as a result of the ministrations of the herbalist.

But this situation was far more serious than that.

When Liz first showed up, Michael rallied. The two comforted each other and then, to celebrate his 35th birthday, they shared his favorite dessert, a three-layer carrot cake with butter. According to a member of Michael's entourage, he really got into eating the cake. This was a relief to everyone around him. In the previous six days he had lost nine pounds, and he did not have weight to lose. Michael reverted to his old self under Liz's benign influence. She could get him through the toughest situations.

Four months later, when Michael would undergo a strip-search at Neverland, he would stare throughout the ordeal at a picture of Liz he propped up for support and encouragement, according to biographer Christopher Andersen. At any rate, that next day in Singapore he wanted to take Liz and hubby Larry on a tour of the city's vast zoological gardens. But in this plan he was thwarted when the city refused to close the facility so Michael and his guests could have the place all to themselves.

Michael's revived mood carried over to that night, when 40,000 ecstatic fans jammed the National Stadium in Singapore for his concert. At the midpoint of the concert, Michael's band surprised him when they broke into singing "Happy Birthday."

The fans quickly got into it and took up singing to Michael as well. Liz Taylor blew him a kiss from her VIP seat. One of Michael's insiders told the news media that everyone had Liz Taylor to thank for Michael's improved condition. She had imparted to him the courage and fortitude to carry on with his world tour.

———————————

Less than 24 hours later, Michael Jackson collapsed in his dressing room at National Stadium shortly before he was scheduled to step out on stage. This is not surprising when you take into account his rapid weight loss during the previous week and the fact that, after gorging with Liz on his birthday carrot cake, he reverted to not eating. Liz coaxed him to at least eat the specially prepared fruit dishes she had instructed his personal chef to prepare, but he refused to do so. He told Liz that just the thought of food and eating made him feel sick.

Liz had planned to stay with Michael only a few days until he got back on his feet. Her original plan had called for her to remain at his side during his concert appearances in Singapore and then in Taiwan. But now she decided to stay longer, if necessary, until Michael shaped up and started to regain his strength by eating or, alternatively, until he placed himself in the care of medical professionals.

Before he collapsed in his dressing room at the stadium minutes before going on stage, Michael had complained about severe headaches. He was also vomiting again and experiencing dizziness. He had apparently pulled out of his suicidal depression only to fall into the clutches of debilitating migraine headaches.

To make matters worse, he had fainted a few times

over the past week, so when he passed out in his dressing room, Liz, concerned to the utmost, insisted that he go to the hospital for a brain scan. She promised to accompany him and did so the following afternoon in order to get him to take proper care of himself. They went to Mount Elizabeth Hospital for an MRI scan. Liz rode to the hospital with Michael in a white van with curtains over the windows. She stayed with Michael at the hospital for the full two hours he was there. Then they rode together back to the hotel. Michael entered the hotel through the kitchen to avoid public exposure and the reporters massed out front.

As they walked through the kitchen, a visibly weak Michael leaned on Liz's shoulder. Later Michael's personal physician, Dr. David Forecast, reported that the results of Michael's medical tests were completely normal, including the brain scan. Once again Liz stayed right by Michael's side as he took to his bed once more. But even she couldn't clear up the malaise he'd fallen into.

He told one friend: "I feel like I'm in the middle of the worst nightmare of my life and I can't wake up. I feel like everyone in the world hates me now — and it's tearing my heart to shreds."

As far as nightmares go, Michael had gotten a taste of them two years earlier when his sister LaToya published her autobiography and, in the same year, author J. Randy Taraborrelli published his book,

Michael Jackson: The Magic and the Madness.

Michael was reported to have offered his sister serious money not to publish her unflattering book. He also scrambled seriously to get his hands on a copy of the book's galleys before its publication. He succeeded in neither. But it is interesting to note, in light of the eventual resolution of the potential Jordie Chandler sexual molestation suit, that Michael's solution to a problem was to throw money at it.

He did the same with author Taraborrelli and his unauthorized biography. The literary agent for Mr. Taraborrelli, Bart Andrews, headquartered in Los Angeles, told the press that Michael offered just under $2 million to have the author pull the book back from publication. Taraborrelli refused. According to agent Bart Andrews, Mr. Taraborrelli stated straightaway, "I won't be bought off."

Why was Michael so eager to stop publication of Mr. Taraborrelli's *Michael Jackson: The Magic and the Madness*? In April of 1991, Michael's mother Katherine obtained an advanced copy of the book. She was devastated by it, breaking down into tears and sobbing and gasping for air. She summoned Michael to the family home in Encino and begged him to do something. Katherine had been driven to hysteria by the book's revelations.

What were some of them?

Sample these assertions, according to Taraborrelli. The book:

◾ Revealed, just as LaToya's book had, that father Joe Jackson administered many savage beatings to his boys, but that he was especially brutal to Michael.

◾ Claimed that Michael had an odd relationship

with diminutive Emmanuel Lewis, the star of the hit show Webster. Emmanuel's mother put an abrupt halt to this relationship when she discovered that Michael and Emmanuel had checked into a hotel as father and son.

■ Detailed how Michael was traumatized as a young boy by the wild womanizing of his father and his brothers during the years when they all toured as the Jackson 5 and later as The Jacksons. This was reputed by the book to be the source of Michael's problems in relating to women, since he had seen so many of them compromised and degraded.

■ Disclosed that Michael was traumatized at age 15 when a family member introduced two prostitutes into his hotel room and locked the door on all three of them. Neither the call girls nor Michael has ever discussed the incident, but the book posed an educated guess that Michael was still a virgin where women were concerned.

■ Divulged that Michael is a lonely recluse who often sleeps on the floor rather than in bed and is in the habit of outfitting five female mannequins in his bedroom in chic and expensive designer clothes. As he dressed these mannequins he conversed with them extensively, according to the book.

When Michael saw how upset and unhinged his mother was by this book, he at first tried legal pressure to have the book withdrawn from publication. When that tactic didn't work, he tried to buy out the author with the nearly $2 million payoff mentioned earlier. Neither strategy worked, and the book was indeed published.

In tandem with sister LaToya's allegations in her

autobiography, this biography by Taraborrelli sharply changed the image of the Jackson family and of Michael Jackson, superstar. Still, Michael's fans were not put off by any of the sensational charges in either book. Yet Michael did confide his anger and misgivings about Mr. Taraborrelli's book to a friend. He told the friend, "This book is the worst thing ever to happen to me."

That was true only for a short time.

In less than two years he found himself in Taiwan in the midst of the child molestation scandal that would torpedo his career and leave his life listing and taking on water.

———

Meanwhile, back in Asia, Michael had left Singapore and traveled to the next destination on his world tour for Dangerous. He had flown to Taipei and settled into a luxurious suite at The Grand Formosa Regent Hotel. Liz Taylor and husband Larry Fortensky moved into another plush suite at the hotel. Both accommodations were provided free to Michael by the management. Under Liz's steady guidance and love, Michael had seemed to stabilize somewhat. She was urging him to eat and he was doing as she requested.

But then the Jackson family showed up. This was not what Michael needed, as even a quick scan of his sister LaToya's autobiography or a breezy read of Taraborrelli's *Michael Jackson: The Magic and the Madness* would convince anyone.

Before the Jackson family left for the Far East to see and comfort Michael, they had held a press conference in Los Angeles to express their support for him. At the press conference, mother Katherine was emphatic that her son would not do anything sexually to molest a child. Michael had been raised as a devout Jehovah's Witness, she asserted, and she was absolutely certain that her son was innocent of the charges and allegations hurled at him. Michael's brother Jermaine was also very voluble at the press conference. He especially decried the rumors that his brother Michael was gay, saying they weren't true and that Michael was into girls but was just very shy, withdrawn, private, reserved and extremely sensitive.

When the Jackson family arrived in Taiwan, they stayed in a separate hotel a few miles away from the one where Michael, Liz and husband Larry were staying. The Jacksons set up camp in The Sherwood, another deluxe hotel. Liz Taylor and Katherine Jackson did not care one whit for each other. Before the Jacksons even arrived, Liz had reportedly criticized Michael's mother in the press. She said that Katherine Jackson should have flown to her son's side the moment the crisis broke. She also said that the televised press conference the Jacksons had held in Los Angeles to express family support for Michael was not enough. Liz was reported to have told a friend, "The Jacksons' press conference was too little, too late. They should all have been on a plane immediately to be with him. A mother's place is by her son's side."

It is easy to imagine how this sat with Katherine

Jackson, the iron willed matriarch and control fanatic. Jackson insiders say Katherine had never liked Liz. She had never approved of the prominent place Liz played in her son Michael's life. She felt usurped by Liz. So naturally, in Taipei, Katherine avoided any event where she was likely to encounter the world famous actress and her husband.

And how did Liz react the next day when Katherine announced that the entire Jackson family would convene for a powwow and lunch? She booked the first flight out of Taipei back to Los Angeles and departed with husband Larry and her bodyguard in under three hours. This was astonishing for Elizabeth Taylor. She travels with a small Matterhorn of luggage and it usually takes her at least three hours just to have maids help pack half her bags. But somehow she pulled everything together and was airborne for LAX in under two hundred minutes.

This didn't sit well with Michael Jackson's entourage. His advisers rightly felt that Liz had healed Michael enough for him to go on with his tour. One employee said: "Those of us working with Michael wish she'd stayed. If she'd remained with us until his Tokyo concert, we would all have heaved a sigh of relief. Liz was the glue that held Michael together. His mother and the rest of the Jackson family don't have the same kind of influence with him. Liz was there with him when he had the migraines in Singapore. And she counseled him like a mother about the need to think positively, and to eat the healthy foods his chef was preparing. Michael responded to her concerns and things began to go much more smoothly. But when Katherine and the family came on the scene, Liz was shunted aside."

After Liz fled the scene, insiders revealed that Michael spent most of his time playing video games in his hotel room. He started acting funny again, disoriented and crippled and curled inward with worry. He decided to go shopping at a Toys"R"Us store and an incident resulted. A crowd gathered and pushing and shoving began between Michael's bodyguards and local press reporters. One guard got cut in the dustup. He had a gash on his head. Michael was outwardly unharmed, but it is interesting that even alone, without one of his special friends as an excuse, the first thing he did when distressed out of his mind was to go to a toy store.

Before Liz Taylor left, she urged Michael to visit Taiwan's outstanding National Palace Museum. But mother Katherine had other plans for her troubled son. She wanted him to see a Buddhist nun she had met years earlier on a trip to Taiwan. The nun was known as the "Mother Teresa of Asia." Katherine was convinced that this mystical nun could spiritually lift her son. But it seems Michael did neither, instead withdrawing back into his shell.

His advisers and handlers believed the price of the Jacksons showing up had cost them the ministrations to their star of the truly nurturing and helpful Elizabeth Taylor. She had made Michael much happier than his family did. The very night the Jacksons arrived in Taiwan marked the first night Elizabeth Taylor had missed a Michael Jackson concert since she'd flown to his bedside in Singapore.

The following morning she was gone. It seems likely that Michael had during the years of his tight friendship with Liz confided in her his anguished feelings about his parents and his siblings.

Sister LaToya said it best: "I'm very surprised my mother didn't go to Michael sooner. I felt she should have been there before Elizabeth because, after all, she is his mother."

Michael would soldier on to his tour dates in Tokyo. He was hugely popular in Japan. Six years earlier, his tour there for Bad had grossed more than $20 million alone. The album had sold 20 million copies worldwide. It was the second highest grossing album in history, exceeded only by Michael's monstrous and still unmatched pop culture triumph Thriller, which had sold the humongous sum of 40 million copies. But this wasn't the Thriller tour. This wasn't the tour for Bad either. This was the tour for the ominously named Dangerous.

Still, Michael Jackson had achieved his boyhood goal — he was the most popular entertainer the world had ever seen and the greatest solo act in history.

Yet he was miserable, the material prince and the spiritual pauper all rolled into one.

And in a few short weeks, he was headed for a Mexican standoff with his own demons — a showdown with self he couldn't possibly win.

"I can't bear any more!" — Michael Jackson to those present in his hotel suite in Mexico City November 8, 1993.

CHAPTER 6

While Michael retreated into a shell in Taiwan, events moved along back in L.A. At first it appeared that Michael's massive public relations machine would put the Chandlers in the spin cycle but good. The idea was that they would come out disoriented, reeling, and grateful just to collapse. According to this wishful scenario, they would cease and desist with their threatened legal actions and the Michael Jackson merry-go-round would continue.

This seemed reasonable, since Anthony Pellicano's counteroffensive was working at first. The issue of People magazine that came out on Michael's 35th birthday, August 29, 1993, stated that he had been cleared by Los Angeles police and the district attorney's office to continue his world tour for Dangerous. Police officials stated that they had no grounds for arresting Michael. They had found no basis on which to take him up on criminal charges. As things stood, it was Michael's word against that of a 13-year-old boy. There was no hard evidence against Michael Jackson as yet. One Los Angeles social worker told reporters it was unfair that Michael Jackson was being tried and found guilty in certain non-judicial circles when he hadn't yet even been charged with a crime.

The article in People mentioned that Michael was reported to be willing to pay $350,000 to the Chandlers as an expedient to avoid any more negative publicity. The People article also stated that police were investigating potential plaintiff Jordie Chandler's dentist father, Evan, for alleged extortion. This last investigation would have been initiated as a result of the Anthony Pellicano counteroffensive.

The Pellicano Plan wasn't all that was going in Michael's favor. Pellicano was an expert at audio recording. He claimed that he had taped conversations in which Evan Chandler allegedly proposed that Michael could avoid further unpleasantness with the Chandlers over alleged sexual misconduct with son Jordie. According to Pellicano, all Michael would have to do is put up $20 million to back four films based on screenplays to be written by him, Evan Chandler.

But this full-time dentist and aspiring screenwriter was not a patsy. He publicly denied ever trying to extort money from Michael Jackson. Evan Chandler stated, "I'm not looking for a dime. I'm just looking for Michael Jackson to leave my son alone."

When quizzed about Pellicano's extortion accusations about him, Evan Chandler countered: "Money never came up until Mr. Pellicano brought it up."

Michael himself was shaky, despite his brother Jermaine's statements to the press that Michael was A-OK and ready to boogie. We saw in the last chapter that Michael had sought to console himself on the departure from Taiwan of Liz Taylor and husband Larry by going on a shopping binge at a Toys"R"Us store. This is the $4,500 shopping orgy that precipitated a riot in which one of Michael's guards received a gash on the head. That very same night in Los Angeles during the MTV Awards ceremony, the mood of the celebrities favored Michael by a wide margin. Evan Chandler was seen as an extortionist. Christopher Andersen, in his book *Michael Jackson: Unauthorized*, reports that Sharon Stone even said that night for attribution: "I firmly believe that if this family has — or ever had . . . evidence of abuse, it would have surfaced by now. All I know is that if a child of mine had been abused, I would not have been making deals."

These remarks were a bit precipitate, but celebrities are not trained, like lawyers, to reserve judgment until the situation becomes clearer. They more often rush in where angels fear to tread.

Shortly thereafter, the Chandlers became clients of lawyer Gloria Allred, who publicized and politicized the case extensively with press interviews. She was well known for winning cases with political and societal overtones that concerned underdogs, and she'd scored many coups for women's rights in litigation.

She promptly announced that her new client Jordan Chandler was ready to go to trial against Michael Jackson. What's more, she was ready to hit the barricades on behalf of the Chandlers and turn them into a political correctness social crusade. She denigrated people who had come out in support of Michael Jackson before the full set of facts could be settled upon. In her favor, Allred was useful for the counterspin she provided to the slanted information she said was being promulgated by security consultant Anthony Pellicano.

Yet Gloria Allred wasn't destined to remain on the Chandler team for long. What happened was simply this: Evan Chandler and his estranged wife June buried the hatchet and combined forces on behalf of son Jordie. They stopped battling over custody and related issues, deciding that they wanted money paid to Jordie to cover the psychotherapy he'd need. They also wanted a trust fund established for their son.

The parents did not want to be turned into the poster family for a crusade centered on the rights of the underdog led by attorney Gloria Allred, who thought that emphasizing monetary damages was inappropriate and gave the wrong impression. She thought it was more important for Jordan Chandler to receive legal redress and moral and social support than to receive a monetary settlement making him comfortable for life. She wanted Jordie to be seen as successful for speaking out against possible sexual interference at the hands of an adult so that other children who were victimized in the same or similar ways would follow his example. But Jordan Chandler's parents did not especially want him further traumatized by a court appearance and trial, which psychiatrists advised them could be harmful to the boy.

This stand by Allred prompted the Chandlers to

put their case against Michael Jackson on behalf of son Jordie back in the hands of lawyer Larry R. Feldman. He was the attorney who'd first approached the Jackson camp back on August 4 in the meeting in the penthouse at the Westwood Marquis Hotel as the legal representative of Evan and Jordie Chandler. More importantly now, attorney Feldman was reserved with the press and far less a social and political crusader than Gloria Allred. But he was steely and determined and smart. He resolved to press the case against Michael Jackson, criminal if necessary, civil in order to win reparations. Take your pick, Michael Jackson.

Somehow, Michael, as smart as ever, knew that this mess was not going to go away as quickly as precious little Tinker Bell could whisk up into the air and disappear. Michael's intelligence was not an educated one, but his instincts for business and for promotion were legendary. He had street smarts to burn, just what you'd expect from someone off the hardscrabble streets of a town as rough and ornery as Gary, Indiana, wide-open, violent, and nicknamed "Sin City."

And Michael was right.

He was in big trouble that would only grow more serious over the next three months.

━━━━━━━━━━

Michael Jackson was legendary for his secretiveness. Yes, he considered himself one of the great self-promoters of the 20th century. Yes, like

Madonna and other publicity junkies, he planted
stories and acted outrageous to gain attention. He
kept his face and his words before the public by
seeming to be caught unaware and overheard in
private, when all the while the whole story, photos
included, would have been planted by him in the
appropriate media outlet. Michael played this game
like the maestro he was, up there with the best
of them, like his friend Andy Warhol or like
Salvadore Dali or Liberace. He knew how to sculpt
eccentricity, canned and calculated, into a great and
looming public image.

But Michael never figured this self-nurtured
publicity monster was about to turn on him and bite
him in the butt quite the way it was about to in the
fall of 1993. One thing he had always insisted on
— when Michael Jackson hired someone, including
musicians and backup singers and all members of his
entourage on world tours, that person had to sign a
confidentiality agreement. What he or she saw or
heard while in the employ of the Gloved One had to
remain with them forever. They had to take this
information with them right to the grave or suffer
the consequences at the hands of Michael's
saber-toothed lawyers and security consultants and
advisers. Michael built a phalanx around him of
silenced "help" like a grand potentate or absolute
monarch, just as though he took his title as the King
of Pop quite royally and literally.

But that autumn of his discontent, that dreadful
fall of 1993, this fortress of silence surrounding him
was breached time and again. People talked. The
Mafia and the underworld had always fascinated

Michael. He had even performed in videos dressed as a gangster. His justly famous imitation of Frank Sinatra, the Chairman of the Board, Old Blues Eyes, had just the right smidgen of the underworld and Damon Runyon about it to give it the patina of the Syndicate. So like all half-grown people, Michael was mightily impressed by the renowned Mafia code of omerta, or silence no matter the cost. His staff didn't share his enthusiasm for this code of silence. Some saw it as being so much like the code of denial and silence germane to the dysfunctional family, which is usually full of tight-lipped but badly battered — verbally, psychologically, and physically — children.

But the parents of one child who considered himself abused weren't going to remain silent.

Back in Los Angeles on September 14, 1993, attorney Larry R. Feldman filed suit against Michael Jackson on behalf of Jordan Chandler. The suit charged Michael with sexual battery, seduction, willful misconduct, intentional infliction of emotional distress, negligence and fraud. The suit laid out details of the sexual misconduct Michael Jackson was accused of, including fellating and masturbating the plaintiff, and having the plaintiff fondle and caress Michael's breasts while Michael brought himself to sexual climax manually. The suit also alleged that Michael manipulated Jordie emotionally by faking despair and grief when the youngster resisted Michael's sexual advances. There was no ambiguity in the language of the suit when it came to Michael Jackson's motives and purposes. It held, as stated earlier, that Michael pursued his agenda with Jordie in order to satisfy his lusts and sexual desires.

Next day, omerta, Michael Jackson style, took a beating. Mark Quindoy and his wife Faye spoke out to reporters in the Philippines. They gave quotes from their detailed diaries about activities they had observed involving Michael Jackson and young boys during the years when they worked at Neverland Ranch. L.A. police officials flew to Manila to interview the Quindoys about Michael Jackson and alleged inappropriate behavior the Quindoy couple had observed him engaged in with young boys at the ranch in Santa Ynez.

Mark Quindoy had come right out and said to reporters that he had seen Michael Jackson molest several children. During the time Quindoy was employed by Michael Jackson, he served as manager of the Neverland Ranch while his wife served simultaneously as the chef. It was reported that both Quindoys had passed lie detector tests administered by the Los Angeles Police Department.

Interestingly, the Quindoys, at the time Los Angeles police officials interviewed them in Manila, were still in a dispute with the Jackson camp over the sum of $283,410 in overtime pay. By taking a stand against Michael's interests, the Quindoys jeopardized the possibility of ever receiving this money. So why would they do this? In Mark Quindoy's own words: "We quit when we could no longer stand what we were seeing." He even went further than this in his statements, adding, "My wife and I have every reason to believe this kid is telling the truth." The kid Mark Quindoy referred to was Jordie Chandler.

Anthony Pellicano fired back at the Quindoys with both guns blazing. Remember, he had already portrayed the Chandlers as a family trying to extort $20 million from Michael Jackson. Perhaps following the philosophy of the more, the merrier, he now characterized the Quindoys as "failed extortionists."

Hurling this insult at the Quindoys didn't have the intended effect. On September 28, the Quindoys filed a criminal libel suit, naming Michael Jackson and Anthony Pellicano as the offending parties.

"I have never tried to extort money from anyone," Mark Quindoy said. He added, "All we're trying to get is unpaid overtime." He referred to the $283,410 in dispute. In firing back at Pellicano, Mark Quindoy sounded a lot like dentist and father Evan Chandler when he responded in a similar manner a short time earlier to the same charge from the same source.

A pattern was developing that did not work in Michael Jackson's favor.

_____

When Michael Jackson had finished his concert in Moscow, he went on to Israel. Not surprisingly, in Israel, a country where religious fervor runs high, he met with public censure. The worldwide headlines had splashed his troubles into every nook and cranny of the globe. Rabbis and other religious leaders in Israel did not approve of the charges against Michael or the way he was handling them.

When Michael attempted to visit the Wailing Wall, a shouting crowd of worshippers forced him to retreat. This was sad and regrettable when you consider Michael's early training in the faith of the Jehovah's Witnesses. But, then again, Michael was now displaying that telltale hallmark of the addict and the talented brat spoiled by fawning lackeys and other sycophants. He was being defiant. He was traveling on tour with two new special friends, even as the allegations of 13-year-old Jordie Chandler held the news media around the world in thrall.

He was accompanied to the Wailing Wall by 9-year-old Eddie Cascio and his older brother, Frank, all of 13. Both boys were from New Jersey and Michael had met them through their father, a member of the staff at the Helmsley Palace Hotel in New York, where Michael used to stay frequently in a penthouse suite.

Their father has since opened his own restaurant, and he always insisted that he and his wife saw nothing wrong with their boys keeping company with Michael, who sometimes took them to the Neverland Ranch and to Las Vegas and to Disneyland. This treatment and its attendant itinerary seemed in fact to be a kind of standard Grand Tour that Michael Jackson treated his special friends to. But when Michael Jackson, world's most famous entertainer, tried to approach the Wailing Wall wearing makeup and holding hands with these two young Cascio boys, the Israeli religious worshippers were having none of it.

Yet that rejection didn't extend to the concert

crowds. Both concerts in Tel Aviv were sold out, and the crowds both nights were loud and appreciative. Michael outwardly seemed unaffected by his rejection at the Wailing Wall. His insides were something else again, as would be clear shortly. He seemed to be flouting conventional morality in the way he was sashaying around with these two adolescent boys. Maybe he just wanted to show that he kept company with such boys without regard for the danger it placed him in professionally or to defy any silly gossip or self-indignation on the part of uptight people. Or maybe he just considered himself above all criticism and intended to buy his way out of the Jordie Chandler mess and trust that all the bad publicity would evaporate into the clouds.

In either case he was wrong — and his actions were stupid.

When he finished his second concert in Tel Aviv, he flew with the Cascio boys to Elizabeth Taylor's side. She was vacationing at her fabulous retreat in Gstaad, Switzerland. Of course Michael was in his element. He had a mother surrogate handy and he had two ready and willing playmates not yet old enough to shave.

What more could he want?

Toys, of course. So he took the Brothers Cascio on a shopping spree and they brought lots of toys and goodies back to Liz's chalet.

There they had multiple water fights and pillow fights and played lots of video games and listened to CD's and romped in pajamas and slippers.

Little did Michael realize he was only weeks away from a set of paper slippers and a place on the flight deck in a world-class rehab named for another famous angel of mercy, Florence Nightingale.

———

While Michael Jackson was still on his Dangerous tour, the police in Los Angeles were busy. On November 8, a whole raft of policemen and police investigators descended on Michael Jackson's boyhood home in Encino, Hayvenhurst, which was still the Jackson family seat. After all, Michael Jackson had lived there, with his parents, until he was 30 years old.

He had only left after a famous confrontation with raging bull of a father, Joseph, his lifelong tormentor and nemesis. One day at a family barbecue Joseph had lost it as Michael mooned about the yard and pool area with a young, blond and blue-eyed male friend. Enraged, Joseph had got in Michael's face and demanded to know what the story was. Were the rumors true? Was he gay? What was with the young pretty boy friend? Why didn't he like girls? Where were his girlfriends? Why was it always boys? Blond boys? Blue-eyed boys? Why, why, why? Joseph wanted to know.

Before Michael, embarrassed and appalled, could respond to his father's rage, Joseph turned on the young visitor and insisted that he leave. He did and, shortly thereafter, so did Michael. The simple response for Michael to this kind of barbaric behavior on the part of dear old dad was to buy the Neverland Ranch for $17 million.

When the 16-person strong contingent from the L.A. Police Department showed up at Hayvenhurst on that November day, all of the Jacksons were away. The police officials confronted a security guard with the official court-ordered search warrant, which was very detailed. The Jackson family was in Phoenix, Arizona, that day attending the funeral services for Katherine's father Samuel, who'd died at the age of 100. Michael, significantly, did not return to the States for his grandfather's funeral. He was too afraid that if he set foot in the territorial United States he would be placed immediately under arrest. So he stayed away on the Dangerous tour.

That family funeral for grandfather Samuel, or anything else, did not stand in the way of the LAPD. They went to work searching Hayvenhurst, looking for evidence to be used against Michael Jackson in a possible upcoming prosecution based on the child molestation allegations. The search warrant was specific and all-encompassing. The police were to look for, among other things:

■ Any photographs, slides, negatives or video recordings of male juveniles, dressed, nude and/or in sexually explicit poses.

■ Any undeveloped film.

■ Diaries, telephone books, address books, correspondence or other writings tending to identify juveniles who have been victims of sexual abuse.

■ To photograph the interior and exterior of the location for identifying purposes and to corroborate witness statements and descriptions.

■ Items of identification.

The warrant listed even more possible evidence to

look for, examine and collect. There were so many police officers combing Hayvenhurst that they seemed to be bumping into each other in their zeal to check out Michael's 1,000-square-foot bedroom and playroom. At the end of the day they carted off 40 to 50 boxes filled with notebooks, files, documents and photographs. They took away with them photos of Michael with young boys, even though the photos were not sexually suggestive, let alone explicit, and in all the shots the boys and Michael were fully dressed. Still, the police took them away in their fleet of unmarked vehicles when they left after searching for hours.

The LAPD were there so long that a call was placed by the security personnel to Arizona, and Katherine Jackson caught the first flight back to L.A. accompanied by sons Randy and Tito and eldest daughter Rebbie. But when the Jacksons got there, there was nothing they could do about the search but stand by, hands on hips, fuming. You can imagine how surprised jaded LAPD cops must have been to discover in Michael's bedroom six mannequins dressed in flapper outfits from the Roaring Twenties, not to mention seeing over 50 dolls in Michael's room, many of them undressed.

Mother Katherine Jackson was still anguished days later. She vented to a friend, "We've been at the house every day for months. And they choose a moment we're away — at a funeral — to raid our home. I feel like we've been violated!"

When word of this police raid and search reached Michael, he was on tour in Mexico City. He could not have been pleased to learn that the Los Angeles policemen searching his old bedroom/playroom in the family mansion had even broken open his personal safe. It was a 150-pound, 25-by-20 inch steel safe lodged in one of his closets. Inside the safe, after the cops pried it open with crowbars, they found nothing but four pages of handwritten notes and an empty lockbox, hardly a great haul for a prosecutor to gloat over.

Still, there would be later debates about just what the cops found in their three searches: the one at Neverland Ranch on August 21, the one at the Century City condo that same fateful August day, and the one on November 8 at Jacko's boyhood home, Hayvenhurst. They had also conducted a fourth search, at Michael's villa at the Mirage in Las Vegas.

That day at Hayvenhurst the cops also found a door in the wall of Michael's room that led to a secret passageway to the gardens outside the home. The passageway's walls were lined with shelves holding children's books.

In Mexico City, awash in his sense of outrage and violation, Michael must have felt like a drowning man. He must have wished for a secret passageway that would lead him out of the mess that was closing in around him like the walls in that old Flash Gordon reel where Ming the Merciless plans to crush the life out of the great crusader for truth and good. But, unlike the ever resourceful Flash Gordon, Michael must have felt like there would be no way out for him.

He was losing his grip.

It's easy to imagine that he felt like an abandoned

child caged in a hall of mirrors with brightly lighted and harshly flashing red signs reflected everywhere and screaming, "No Exit, No Exit, No Exit!"

———————

On November 8, 1993, Michael Jackson clinically cracked up in Mexico City. The news of the police raid on Hayvenhurst that day sent him flying over the edge. The image of cops crawling all over his old bedroom/playroom back in Encino was too much for him. The sense of violation and outrage must have triggered memories of other savage personal violations and humiliations from childhood coursing through his mind, tearing apart any lingering sense of serenity. He went to pieces. He fell apart. His mind jumped the trolley tracks. He suffered a total psychotic break with reality and went off his head.

For weeks, Michael Jackson had lived in clenched fear that the police investigation back in California of child molestation charges against him would result in his imminent arrest. He pictured himself led away in handcuffs and thrown into a cell with rough convict types. Feelings of guilt at such shaming images of his fallen self must have kicked up strictures inculcated in him in endless sessions in the Kingdom Hall meetings of Jehovah's Witnesses. He might well have suffered auditory hallucinations, hearing the voices of angry preachers calling hellfire for his sins, real and imagined, down around his head. So he sought relief from his rioting nerves in more and more drugs. He went on a drug binge, in fact, for two solid weeks leading up to his nervous breakdown. He overindulged in the use of both the painkiller Percodan and the tranquilizer Valium, a treacherous pharmaceutical cocktail if taken together in too heavy doses.

Insiders forced to cope with Michael in the grip of his complete psychotic break with reality told of its horrors. He screamed over and over again that he wished he were dead, just as he had in Bangkok two and half months earlier. But now his cries were even more desperate. He scared his bodyguards and advisers even more now than he had back then, when head of security Bill Bray had placed Michael under a 24-hour, around-the-clock suicide watch. Michael had ensconced himself in his hotel suite in Mexico City at the swanky Hotel Presidente. He was living desperately in self-imposed exile, fearing every new development in the police investigation back home. When he got word on November 8 that the cops had tossed and ransacked his childhood home in search of incriminating evidence against him, Michael lost it completely. The damage to the posh hotel suite was devastating.

Among other manifestations of Michael's nervous breakdown are these:

■ He began to pace his hotel suite and alternately laugh raucously and cry hysterically.

■ He rammed his head against a wall so hard that he indented the plaster.

■ He vomited all over the carpet.

■ He dashed off nearly incoherent love notes while talking to himself.

■ He scattered these notes around the suite.

■ He scrawled nonsensical graffiti on the walls of the suite.

When Michael's rampage came to an end, the tab for the damage done to the suite amounted to $3,000. The suite itself was so luxurious that it cost $5,000 a night to rent. He'd trashed the place in the best style of the displeased and deranged rock star. But it was much sadder and much more tragic than a drunken or drugged-up tantrum. Michael's mind had dissolved to mush. He had scribbled on the walls like a Montessori kid run amok in creative arts class. He had shouted and mumbled and blabbered away to himself, none of it really intelligible, most of it just gibberish. He may have had a messianic delusion lacing through his psyche when he started writing "I love you" over and over on notepaper and then scattering the notes around the suite. He is reported to have smiled after he did this and said, "It's true, you know. I do love you. You're all my children."

The stadium twice being filled to capacity in Tel Aviv for his concerts had countered his rejection in Israel at the Wailing Wall two months earlier. The Israeli fans had screamed and stomped their approval. Some fans had even testified that Michael Jackson was a kind of Messiah. This was not an illogical conclusion to draw from the performances on the Dangerous tour. The song lyrics and the stage imagery Michael employed on the Dangerous tour were openly and heavily geared to religious themes. It was clear to anyone sentient that a child as bright and sensitive as Michael Jackson had been would not easily or lightly cast off the injunctions and inhibitions hammered into him as a child by the Jehovah's Witnesses.

Surely being in the Holy Land and being

alternately rejected as a defiled heathen at a sacred shrine and then exalted as a savior by nearly 200,000 screaming fans would further widen the crippling fissure in Michael's mind and psyche. Was he a benefactor to children the world over? Or was he an abomination and danger to every child unlucky enough to come into contact with him? This was undoubtedly the war being waged in Michael's heart and mind.

He was a man pulled in two opposite directions. In Mexico City he had indulged his pleasures with special friends again. He was vested somehow in proving that he would not alter his lifestyle or admit in any way, shape, or form that his preference for the company of children, and especially that of young and adolescent boys, was in any way unhealthy, abnormal, or out of line. This duality in Michael's heart, mind and soul had to lead somewhere, and where it led was into a psychotic break with reality that unnerved his entire security staff and his close inner circle of advisers. Mexico City represented for Michael Jackson what addicts call a bottom, meaning he had hit bottom and had no choice now but to seek help.

———

As he had before and would again, Michael Jackson sought the help of Elizabeth Taylor. When he learned that Hayvenhurst had been tossed, to use police lingo, violating Michael's privacy even more severely than it had been violated back in August with the raids and searches on Neverland Ranch and the Century City condo, he called Liz Taylor in Los Angeles at her Bel Air home. He then made an impassioned and nearly hysterical plea for her help. Of course, to her enduring credit, she gave it. Liz Taylor is nothing if not compassionate. She must have been truly frightened for Michael's safety this time. He reportedly told her, "I feel as though I'm drowning." Liz and Larry wasted no time. They packed hurriedly and hired a Learjet to whisk them to Michael's side in Mexico City.

But unfortunately for Michael, he could not simply beam Liz up the way Scotty could do it on Star Trek. This meant that before Liz arrived, Michael flipped out. He went on his crying and laughing jags and trashed his suite. During the interval between calling Liz and her arrival several hours later, he also was sick on the carpets and slammed his head against the wall. After that is when he maniacally wrote the "I love you" notes that marked his utter separation from reality and conviction he was a Messiah-like apostle of love dispatched to spread his message all over the world. While his delusional system was wreaking havoc with Michael's ability to stay in reality, he must have flashed over and over in his mind on the image of seven carloads of LAPD officers and investigators pulling up in Encino and invading every inch of Hayvenhurst.

Michael's escalating drug problem was exasperated in Mexico City when he had to have dental work. A local dentist pulled a left molar and prescribed two medications for Michael. The dentist put him on the painkiller Dolacet and the antibiotic Metronidazole. You don't have to be a doctor or pharmacist to know what kind of fire Michael was playing with by ingesting these two new drugs on top of Percodan and Valium. He must have been as staggered and ready to collapse as a shot fighter about to be knocked unconscious in the waning rounds of a heavyweight fight, because that's exactly what he did. He went into his bedroom and collapsed on the bed, curled up again in the fetal position, his knees tucked up under his chin. That's exactly how Liz Taylor found him when she arrived, again in the middle of the night, just as she had a little over two months earlier in Singapore. To be precise, Liz arrived at one in the morning. She didn't go to bed but instead went right to Michael's suite and entered his bedroom.

She sat by Michael's bedside and held his hand. Tears welled up in her eyes as she soothed Michael's forehead with a damp cloth as he slept soundly. She whispered endearments like "Sleep, my baby. I'm here now." No doubt Liz was appalled by the condition of the wrecked hotel suite, but she focused her attention and her love on Michael.

When he woke up the next morning, he was over the moon to find her there. She calmed him and told him things would be all right. But she also told him that he'd run his string to the end. He had to get professional help for his drug dependence. She herself had done it and so could he. She further shaped him up enough for him to perform on stage that night of November 9 and two nights later, which, ironically enough for someone who liked to dress onstage like a toy soldier and was now officially among the walking wounded, was Veterans Day back in the States. The Veterans Day performance would be Michael's last in public for some time to come.

For, all the while Liz was comforting Michael, she was plotting his escape and what she hoped would be his salvation. She couldn't have failed to notice the wreckage he had reduced his life to. Physically he was a total mess, as well as psychologically and emotionally. And she had only to glance at his suite to note that he had reduced a ritzy penthouse to looking like a junkie's den. According to Andersen, the carpet was stained with vomit and pockmarked with pellets of discarded chewing gum. The walls and even some pieces of furniture were covered with illegible and incoherent scrawl in pen and pencil markings. There was a deep depression in one wall that marked the spot where Michael had bashed his head repeatedly. And everywhere Liz looked, trash was strewn on the floors and on the furniture.

It was time for Michael to join other addicts on the flight deck — that's what they call it in rehab when you enter the induction rooms. It was time for Michael to surrender white satin socks and black patent leather loafers for a pair of paper slippers. It was time for Michael to get real and face down his ever-mounting problems.

Michael's friends and allies would see his next move as healthy and lifesaving, but proof that his troubles were only beginning was present as well.

Because Michael's enemies saw this latest move of his in a different light. They saw it as more avoidance on his part. They saw him dodging the consequences of his actions. To them he was simply flying the coop.

"My son wanted to heal the world. But now Michael needs healing." — Katherine Jackson to daughter LaToya shortly after Michael Jackson canceled his world tour for Dangerous and dropped from public view.

CHAPTER 7

Michael Jackson finished his concert on the night of Veterans Day in the gigantic, 120,000-seat soccer stadium in Mexico City and, still bathed with sweat and exhausted from his performance, he retreated to a subterranean reception room. There he waited anxiously for Liz Taylor, husband Larry Fortensky and Liz's personal bodyguard Moshe Alon, a former Israeli commando. All three arrived shortly after and whisked Michael into a waiting vehicle. They then went straight to the airport. On the tarmac was an MGM Grand Air Boeing 727 that Liz had chartered to take them to London by way of stops in Canada and Iceland to refuel.

Liz, Larry and Moshe Alon had wrapped Michael in towels as they helped him to the vehicle after the concert and then onto the waiting jetliner with its engines idling and ready to go.

They disappeared into the Mexican night. No word of their whereabouts could be gleaned for days. Reporters on all six continents were on the lookout for the most famous entertainer in the world. But not one glimpse of him could be had. He had apparently vanished in an operation characterized by military precision. After all, it was the work of Moshe Alon, following the orders of Liz Taylor. She had managed to persuade Michael to do something about his drug dependence. He had agreed to allow Liz to orchestrate his escape and his rehabilitation.

What happened was this: The MGM Grand Air Boeing 727 was originally scheduled to land in Ireland. But something went wrong with the secret plans. Word reached the occupants of the jetliner that somehow a leak had occurred and there would be a contingent of reporters and media types present when the aircraft put down in the Emerald Isle. So the pilot radioed ahead and asked permission to alter his flight plan and fly instead to Luton Airport, outside London, England. Luton, north of London in the home counties, was not nearly as busy or famous as Heathrow and Gatwick. It was used most often for commercial flights. Landing there would afford more privacy than putting down at either of London's world-class airports. Permission was granted and the Boeing 727 put down at Luton shortly after midnight, local time, on November 13. For nearly six hours the plane sat at one end of a rarely-used and darkened runway. Then it took off again.

But before the plane took wing again it had disgorged the world's most famous entertainer and had replaced him with a look-alike. This was a cloak-and-dagger op in the true sense of the phrase. At Luton plans had been made beforehand for Michael Jackson to be secretly removed from the plane and replaced by a double. That way, as far as customs and immigration officials were concerned, no one had entered Great Britain. The jet simply refueled on a layover and then took off again and flew to Switzerland. When it reached its destination, Liz and Larry deplaned and went to Liz's fabulous chalet in Gstaad. No black man deplaned in Switzerland. It can only be presumed that the Michael Jackson look-alike, dressed exactly as Michael Jackson had been when he left Mexico City nearly 24 hours earlier, remained on board the plane and flew with its pilots to its final destination. But in any case, he was not the real Michael Jackson, even though he had boarded the plane at Luton a few hours earlier, in a clever switch, as though he were.

So what had happened to the real Michael Jackson?

That was revealed a little under a year later, in the summer of 1994, in an interview British bodyguard Steve Tarling gave to the press. In the interview, Tarling said he was the man who took Jacko off the plane at Luton, describing his actions that night. He said that Michael Jackson on his clandestine night flight to rehab was so laced with drugs that he had to be carried from the plane. Tarling said, "I carried him like you would carry a tree trunk. He was like a zombie."

Tarling carried Jackson to a van and then slipped him past customs. He and Liz Taylor then took

Michael to the home of Elton John's manager, John Reid. It had been Elton John who had suggested an alternative to Liz Taylor over the international phone when Michael Jackson refused to follow in the footsteps of Liz and husband Larry Fortensky and check into the Betty Ford Clinic for treatment. Liz and Larry had, of course, met at Betty Ford when both were in recovery. But Michael would not hear of going back to the United States. He feared he would be arrested the minute he set foot in the States.

In fact, Michael Jackson was so afraid of being cuffed and hauled off to jail that he hadn't gone on to the next scheduled destination on the Dangerous tour. He did not want to risk stepping off a plane in Puerto Rico, a United States territory. Things behind him in the United States had heated up. The police had stepped up their investigation of him in Los Angeles and word from that quarter was increasingly worrisome for Jacko.

Larry R. Feldman, the attorney for Jordan Chandler, had filed civil suits against Michael back in September, but he had not stopped his efforts there. When Michael Jackson's lawyers asked for a six-year delay in the civil case until a possible criminal case could be solved, attorney Feldman well realized that the Jackson legal team wanted to drag things out so that the statute of limitations would expire on criminal charges. If that happened, Michael Jackson would be off the hook. That's why Feldman had recently filed papers demanding that Jackson return from his international tour to give the court a deposition. Feldman went even further than that. He requested that the court order the elusive and cagey superstar to make available every piece of paper, whether it was private or public, that had relevance for the case. Among the items Feldman wanted Michael to turn over to the court were:

■ The full telephone records from his various residences and from hotels where he'd stayed while with Jordan Chandler or during the six months when he had close contact with the boy.

■ All employee documents that showed times worked by Neverland Ranch employees and employees at other Jackson residences during the same period of time.

■ All receipts, bills and other documents, like airline tickets or car rental contracts, relevant to the trips Michael took with Jordie, including trips with Jordie's mother and sister Lily.

■ All receipts, credit card bills and documents that showed money spent by Michael on trips with Jordie, such as toy and video store receipts, clothing store receipts and any other such paperwork confirming money spent and gifts bought.

Feldman stated his position at length to the press: "This child needs closure. Jackson's refusal to interrupt his tour to let me interview him, and his efforts to have the case put on hold for six years, amount to him taking the Fifth Amendment. He's not testifying. And he doesn't want anyone else to either. That's an amazing thing for a superstar who claims he's innocent. Innocent people welcome the opportunity to prove their innocence. Innocent people do not scoff at the law and refuse to testify under oath. Innocent people do not ask the court to postpone until the year 2000 the case that is supposed to prove their innocence."

By the middle of November, when Michael fled Mexico City by night, the public relations tide had turned sharply against him. Feldman was proving to be a tough opponent, both in terms of the letter of the law and as a man who knew how to put news spin on his actions. He was frank and direct and effective. He didn't appear calculated.

That was not the perception that developed around Michael Jackson and his advisers and his teams of lawyers. At the end of October, on the 29, only hours before Mischief Night and Halloween, ironically enough, in papers filed in a Los Angeles court, Michael denied absolutely all sex abuse allegations against him and accused Jordan Chandler's dentist father Evan of attempted blackmail.

Of course Michael was still openly admitting that he had lavished gifts and trips on Jordie Chandler and on his mother June and sister Lily. But Michael maintained that all of this was done purely out of friendship, just as he had done the same thing with earlier friends like Emmanuel Lewis, Macaulay Culkin, Sean Lennon, Brett Barnes, Corey Feldman and a few others. In the early days of his public relations counteroffensive, Michael's security consultant, Anthony Pellicano, had induced many of Michael's former special friends to tell the police that Michael had never acted improperly with them, either sexually or any other way. In fact, Macaulay Culkin had been incensed at the Los Angeles police for quizzing him about his friend Michael. Still, despite votes of support in some corners, Michael's

An 11-year-old Michael's already well on the road to fame as the lead singer of the Jackson 5

The young singer seemed happy in the spotlight

Michael, age 16, before going under the surgeon's scalpel

Michael Jackson at the
pinnacle of his fame —
his album Thriller would
become the biggest-selling of all time

Michael gazes adoringly at Bubbles the chimp

On the Victory Tour, Michael wears his trademark sequined glove and his first "new" nose

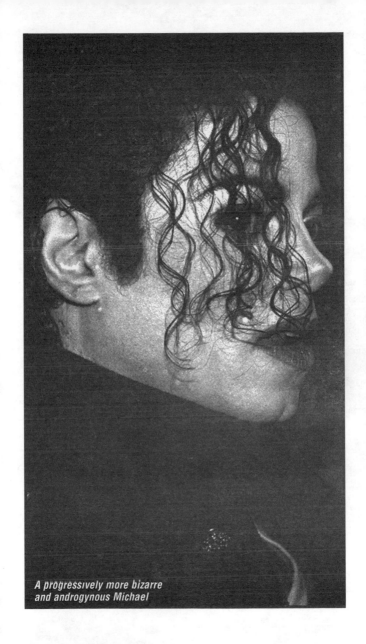

A progressively more bizarre and androgynous Michael

The ever-changing
face of fame

Michael meets a young fan while wearing tape on his collapsing nose

A young fan gives Michael a hug during a performance at an awards ceremony

Michael engages in one of his favorite pasttimes — performing for kids

*The superstar visits Disney World with Macaulay Culkin (above).
Inset: Despite having beautiful Brooke Shields on his arm,
Michael pays close attention to child star Emmanuel Lewis*

Michael with Jordie Chandler, who would later be paid millions to drop sexual molestation charges against the performer

Michael enjoys the kiddie rides with Brett Barnes

One of Michael's fans dresses to resemble the superstar

In a video taken at the Neverland Ranch, Michael, like the Pied Piper, leads the kids to the merry-go-round and they join him for a spin

The video shows Jacko performing to Mary Poppins tunes while his little friends splash in the pool

Top photo: also in the video, Michael stands by the slide as a young, bare-chested boy walks by; above and right: Michael galavants with the young boy on the grounds of his Neverland Ranch

Michael with his bevy of beauties (clockwise from above): Brooke Shields, Diana Ross, Elizabeth Taylor and Madonna

A marriage made in music heaven: Michael with Elvis' daughter, Lisa Marie Presley

Michael and Lisa Marie clowning around during a photo shoot

Michael holds his nose while accompanying Lisa Marie — the marriage would last less than 2 years

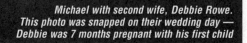

*Michael with second wife, Debbie Rowe.
This photo was snapped on their wedding day —
Debbie was 7 months pregnant with his first child*

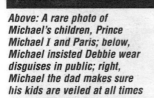

Above: A rare photo of Michael's children, Prince Michael I and Paris; below, Michael insisted Debbie wear disguises in public; right, Michael the dad makes sure his kids are veiled at all times

A progressively more reclusive Jackson shows less and less of his face in public

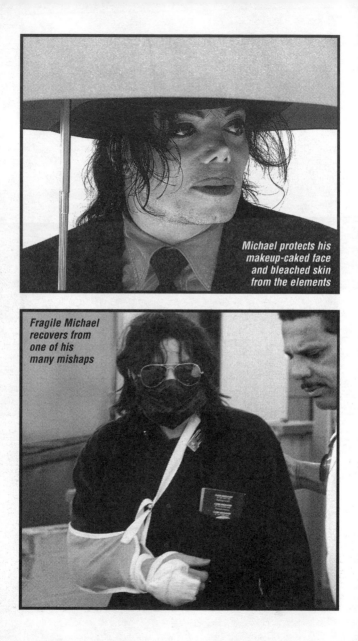

Michael protects his makeup-caked face and bleached skin from the elements

Fragile Michael recovers from one of his many mishaps

Michael confers with American Bandstand legend Dick Clark

A ghost of his former self: An emaciated
Jackson smiles for the camera

GO BACK
TO HELL
MOTTOLA!!

When sales of Michael's most recent album Invincible tanked, he blamed it on a racist conspiracy

Michael buddies up to the controversial Reverend Al Sharpton

Michael in court November 2002, accused of canceling concert appearances

Reading the fine print: Michael holds up a magnifying glass, revealing a bleached and bloated hand

Michael haphazardly dangles his youngest child, Prince Michael II, over the edge of a balcony, 65 feet in the air

Wacko Jacko — always hiding behind a curtain of controversy

refusal to return to the States gave the appearance that he was guilty. No less a friend than Diana Ross gave a statement to the press expressing her concern for Michael and imploring him to return from Mexico City and clear his name.

Michael Jackson's response was to skulk out of Mexico City by night wrapped in towels and a blanket and to retreat to England. One unidentified Los Angeles detective told the press that the LAPD was beginning to fear that it had another Roman Polanski case to contend with. This unnamed detective referred of course to the genius Polish film director who had skipped town when faced with prosecution for having had sex with a 13-year-old girl. Polanski had fled the City of Angels for the City of Light and lived in Paris in self-imposed exile, unable to return to the United States without facing the possibility of arrest. The detective who gave this statement to the press obviously thought that Michael Jackson had also skipped town for good.

But that was not the case.

Michael Jackson was either seriously addicted to drugs or he was using a very clever ruse to buy time and see which way the wind would blow, out of reach of the long arm of United States law enforcement officials.

———

Bodyguard Steve Tarling said that when he boarded the MGM Grand Air Boeing 727 at Luton Airport, he found Michael slumped in his seat apparently asleep. Michael had a red tartan blanket wrapped over his legs and a black hat tilted over his eyes. Liz Taylor woke him and told him he had to get up and move. Tarling testified in his interview that what he saw next shocked him. He said that when Michael's hat fell off revealing his face, it was a pitiful sight. Michael still had red lipstick on and eyeliner and his face was covered with white makeup. Tarling said he looked like a transvestite who hadn't changed his makeup in days. But what really threw the British bodyguard was Michael's nose. He said the tip of Michael's nose was pitch black, the color a scab gets when it is fully formed and mature.

Then when Michael, finally awake after much shaking by Liz Taylor and Michael's personal physician, Dr. David Forecast, tried to rise from his chair, he couldn't make it. His legs gave out and he collapsed. That's when Tarling picked him up and carried him like a baby. Then he and Liz whisked Michael in a nondescript van to the house owned by John Reid, Elton John's manager.

Liz was angered by this last development. She wanted Michael delivered straight into the hands of the staff at Charter Nightingale Clinic, the British analogue to the Betty Ford Clinic. The Charter Nightingale Clinic in central London had started life in the Victorian era as the Florence Nightingale Hospital for Gentlewomen. It had been founded and run by the world famous nurse and angel of mercy in the Crimean War, Florence Nightingale herself.

But Tarling had upset Liz by taking Michael to a private home. Yet Tarling was only doing his duty. He had followed orders from therapist Beauchamp

Colclough and taken Michael to John Reid's house because the press had caught on to Michael's presence and somehow were awaiting his arrival at the clinic in London proper. Liz didn't care. She wanted her darling friend delivered to the clinic as soon as possible. Once arrangements had been made to do so, she left. She then whipped back to the plane waiting on the tarmac at Luton and took off with the Michael Jackson double for Switzerland.

When Liz Taylor called Elton John from Mexico City and explained that she needed to get Michael Jackson into a rehab, and that he wouldn't return to the United States voluntarily, Elton John suggested that Liz get Michael to London and into the hands of the man who had helped Elton get himself clean and sober. That man was Beauchamp Colclough, called "Beechy," the therapist and counselor that ex-addict Elton John thanked for getting him to stop abusing drugs, alcohol and food.

Colclough had helped many other British film, rock and television stars to overcome their addictions, including Eric Clapton. He would put Michael into a 12-step program based on what some people call the Minnesota Method, after the famous rehabilitation center in that state known as Hazelden. When Tarling and Liz got Michael to John Reid's house, Beechy Colclough was waiting there for them. Before Liz would agree to leave, they had to reveal to her their plans for getting Michael into Charter Nightingale Clinic ASAP.

That's how a white ambulance came to back up to the laundry entrance of the world famous clinic in central London a short while later. In the predawn hours, about the time Liz Taylor was flying off to Switzerland with hubby Larry and her beloved Maltese dog, Sugar — and with the Michael Jackson look-alike onboard the Boeing 727 as well — the white ambulance delivered Michael Jackson into rehab. The media gaggle, acting on a tip, had gathered at the front of the Charter Nightingale Clinic. So they had no idea that bottomed-out Michael Jackson was being delivered like a sack of soiled laundry to the back entrance. Over the next several weeks, the Charter Nightingale Clinic refused to answer questions about Jacko. They would neither confirm nor deny that he was a patient at the clinic.

This sent the worldwide media into a frenzy. Newspapers across the world wasted no time mounting massive searches to locate the most famous entertainer in history. One paper's editors even promised a huge reward to anyone who could lead them to Michael Jackson's whereabouts.

When Liz returned to the United States from Switzerland after a short stay there, she would not tell reporters where Michael was. She said that she would continue to remain silent as long as necessary to help Michael. As she had on many other occasions, she said simply, "I love him like a son."

Liz's silence angered Katherine Jackson. As Michael's mother, she felt entitled to know where her son was. Again she felt usurped and upstaged by Liz Taylor, scene stealer extraordinaire. She wanted Liz to break all ties to Michael and to leave him alone to do battle with his demons and to come to terms with his addiction to painkillers. When no trace of Michael showed up, there were stories that newspapers dispatched reporters to check out hotels and hospitals and clinics all over the world. There were even stories of reporters dropping into zoos, Toys"R"Us stores, and amusement parks trying to capture a glimpse of the most notorious overgrown kid in history possibly in search yet again of his lost childhood.

They would have no luck because Michael Jackson was busy mastering the 12 Steps. And it wasn't a new dance or something offered at the Arthur Murray Studios. It was a matter of life and death, or so Michael Jackson's public relations people told the world.

Michael Jackson was participating in group therapy — he was in recovery, big-time.

───

Bodyguard Steve Tarling said that when he and Liz got Michael to Elton John's manager's house, the superstar practically fell out of the van. Tarling stated that Michael sort of slithered out like a corpse. Tarling and Liz had to grab him before he hit the ground. He was rubbery and zonked out and completely unable to look after himself.

But by the time they got the plans all set to take Michael into central London in the white ambulance, he had revived somewhat and was his usual calculating and brilliant self.

Michael had agreed to follow the plans laid out for him by Liz Taylor, but when she left to return to Luton Airport, Beechy Colclough was in charge. And Michael didn't know or trust him. So Michael couldn't know that Colclough was himself a recovered alcoholic and drug addict. Plus, he was an ex-rock musician. All of this would have endeared him to Michael, but of course Michael had no way of knowing this. And in his zapped and drugged-out condition, Michael would probably not have listened well had Beechy tried to win Michael's confidence by telling him his own miraculous life story of recovery and triumph.

This explains why Michael panicked in the back of the ambulance on the way into London when therapist Colclough informed him that in the clinic he would have no contact with the outside world. To this Michael replied: "If I can't use the telephone, I'm calling the whole thing off."

When they got to the clinic, Tarling said Michael started to drift around the exclusive rehab center, asking staff and other patients how you got out of there. Michael had dressed up to leave. He'd even put his signature hat on. But the staff intercepted Michael and got him on an IV drip full of a sedative to ease him off the drugs. This is standard practice when detoxing somebody strung out on painkillers or other drugs.

Pretty soon Michael stopped attempting to leave without permission and settled down. He participated in the clinic's various therapies. He attended group sessions led by Colclough. As with all group therapy sessions in a rehabilitation center, Michael was urged to share his feelings. He did, stating that his childhood had been a nightmare and that he was innocent of the recent accusations hurled against him. He also spoke movingly of how much he longed to have had a real childhood, instead of the gruesome working childhood he had gone through, with much too much exposure to tawdry adult behavior in nightclubs and strip joints.

This talking therapy must have done Michael a world of good. He had taken over an entire floor of the clinic, the way he was used to taking over vast and luxurious hotel suites. That wasn't so odd in the case of the Charter Nightingale Clinic, since it was so posh it might as well have been a top-flight hotel. It was miles above the kind of no-frills, grim and functional rehabilitation center many alcoholics and addicts have sobered up in. There was even a small exercise gymnasium, not that Michael Jackson ever liked to exercise, as he would so bluntly inform that inquisitive publisher nine years later in August of 2002 in Stamford, Connecticut.

Each room in the Charter Nightingale Clinic also had amenities more commonly found in a swanky hotel than in a rehab, including a color television and a radio in a small entertainment center. The place was ·anything but spartan, and it clearly helped Michael, especially in getting him off painkillers and allowing him to share his feelings, to cry, and to vent his anger in a safe environment. But his unmolested stay there didn't last as long as might have been good for him. The reason? You guessed it. The press found him, as they seem always to do.

———

When the media caught on to the fact that Michael Jackson was in the Charter Nightingale

Clinic, Beauchamp Colclough had Steve Tarling sneak Michael back to John Reid's house, where Michael felt much more comfortable anyway. But, as could be expected, now that he was detoxed from sedatives and painkillers, Michael had trouble sleeping. So, as he used to do for years, he filled his sleepless hours with endless phone calls. He called people all over the world at all hours of the day and night. Some of these calls had to do with business, and this would fuel the anger of Michael's detractors maintaining that the whole rehab gambit was a shrewd legal dodge on his part.

At John Reid's house Michael also whiled away many hours watching films. He watched a favorite of his, Whatever Happened to Baby Jane? He also looped several times the John Candy film, Uncle Buck. Then he had a craving to see one of his all-time favorite movies. He wanted to have a video delivered of Gone With the Wind. Tarling put forth a mighty effort to locate a copy, but the closest he could come was to get his hands on a cassette of The Making of Gone With the Wind. When that was all Tarling could come up with, he was impressed with the graciousness Michael exhibited in thanking him for trying so hard.

Tarling would not be the first person to remark on how well-mannered and gracious Michael Jackson could be.

Maybe it was better that Tarling couldn't come up with a copy of Gone With the Wind. Michael might have realized as he watched it that more than Atlanta was burning. He might have felt like Scarlett that all but the land was lost.

You see, while he was hiding in Mexico, wildfires had swept down on the Neverland Ranch. Miraculously, at the last possible moment, the raging forest fires had veered away from Michael's splendid house.

But the real heat was still on Michael Jackson in ways that would incinerate him if he weren't lucky.

"Forget about the superstar, forget about the icon. If he was any other thirty-five-year-old man who was sleeping with little boys, you wouldn't like this guy."
— LaToya Jackson speaking of brother Michael, Tel Aviv press conference, December 8, 1993.

CHAPTER 8

While the flight carrying the zonked Michael Jackson to the Charter Nightingale Clinic in London was still in the air over the North Atlantic, United States officials at San Juan Airport were informed that he might have been whisked out of Mexico to an unknown destination. The officials were waiting to question him in connection with the legal entanglements brewing back in Los Angeles.

Originally Michael had been scheduled to fly to Puerto Rico on November 12, the day after finishing his last performance in Mexico City's huge soccer stadium. But plans changed. Not only was Michael hopelessly addicted to drugs, according to his advisers and fairy godmother Liz Taylor, but he was paralyzed with fear that he would be cuffed and taken into custody the moment he stepped off the plane in Puerto Rico, a United States territory.

So, in the view of Michael's detractors and the Chandlers and their lawyer, Larry R. Feldman, Michael Jackson was playing the artful dodger. They also thought he was playing Jake the Fake with the drug addiction plea. To them he was using it as a convenient coverup to keep him out of the reach of the law. As far as they were concerned, he was, for all intents and purposes, on the lam. But, unlike a poor fugitive, Michael Jackson had lots of swag and could afford to hole up in one of the world's chicest and most private rehabilitation centers.

On December 12, Michael Jackson's public relations representatives released a taped statement from him. In it, among other things, he said: "My friends and doctors advised me to seek professional guidance immediately in order to eliminate what has become an addiction."

Then he explained that he had first used painkillers after his hair and scalp were burned in the fiery accident in 1984 when he was making his spectacular commercial for Pepsi at the Shrine Auditorium in Los Angeles. He further explained that he had again used painkillers, but in an appropriate and reserved manner, after surgery seven months earlier to repair damage incurred 10 years earlier in that original painful accident. But he said that his use of painkillers had grown recently to the point where it was now an addiction for which he had to seek professional treatment.

He added: "I realize that completing this tour is no longer possible, and I must cancel the remaining dates. I know I can overcome the problem and will be stronger for the experience."

This decision to cancel the rest of his world tour for Dangerous, as Michael would shortly learn, would cost him dearly, including facing a $20 million damages suit from the promoter.

About the legal predicament he now found himself in, he said: "As I left on this tour, I had been the target of an extortion attempt and, shortly thereafter, was accused of horrifying and outrageous conduct. I was humiliated, embarrassed, hurt, and suffering great pain in my heart. The pressure resulting from these false allegations, coupled with the incredible energy necessary for me to perform, caused so much distress that it left me physically and emotionally exhausted."

He concluded his taped statement by saying that this legal crisis precipitated his dependence on the drugs to get him through the day and enable him to perform on the tour. But he could no longer do this. He couldn't live this way. He needed professional help. He elaborately thanked Liz Taylor for her intervention on his behalf, and for her abundant love and support. Then he closed, as he almost always did from stage and in press releases, by sending his love out to everyone.

Then, as far as the world was concerned, he vanished.

———

Pepsi immediately canceled Michael Jackson's sponsorship arrangement with them. A spokesperson claimed that the decision to end the company's affiliation with Michael was only natural since the agreement was only for the length of the Dangerous tour and Michael himself had ended the tour, effectively firing himself. But this was just putting cosmetics on the ugly facts. Industry sources said that Pepsi no longer wanted to be associated with a man charged with the alleged sexual molestation of a minor.

Sony took the opposite course of action, supporting their investment. They had announced a few years earlier what was said to be the biggest recording contract in history. The announced figure was a billion dollars, but insiders later disclosed that this figure was based on performance clauses and bonuses and that the actual base amount, absent escalators, was considerably lower than the announced 10-figure deal. It was said that Michael himself, with his acknowledged genius for self-promotion, had engineered and massaged the figure up to a billion dollars.

Certain African-American groups reacted negatively to the news about Pepsi dropping Michael Jackson. There was a sense of outrage that Michael had been dropped so precipitously without having been found guilty of any misdoings, let alone of a criminal offense.

But in general, the public relations tide had turned against Michael. When he hadn't returned to the States but instead holed up in Mexico, hobnobbing with the Mexican president, Carlos Salinas, more people had lent their voices to the chorus calling for Michael to return and clear his name. To this growing number of people Michael Jackson looked guilty through avoidance. This situation wasn't helped when Chandler family lawyer Larry R. Feldman pointed out in a press interview, sarcastically, that it was quite unfortunate that his young client had driven superstar Michael Jackson, 22 years the kid's senior, to drug addiction. Lawyer Feldman also underscored his skepticism, and that of many others, that Michael Jackson could globehop from Asia to Europe to the Near East to South America to promote his latest album. Yet, the brilliant attorney pointed out, Michael Jackson could not find time to return to the U.S. to give a court deposition in response to the criminal and civil suits lodged against him.

Michael Jackson was a maestro of publicity, a grand master of self-promotion, a genius of selling one's self and one's talent, the supreme humanitarian and apostle of universal love and tolerance and understanding. Yet now he was starting to lose a popularity contest to an unknown young boy and his steadfast father and their very able lawyer.

Had he been a stock, Michael Jackson would have gone from blue chip to wastepaper in one quick swipe. This was the beginning of the end of Michael Jackson's reign as the King of Pop.

How could he have let it happen?

———

That was the very question Michael Jackson and his advisers were stuck asking themselves. And, naturally, it led to infighting and dissension. The blame game was on and it was being played with a vengeance. Finger pointing was in fashion in the Jackson camp. Indeed, it was all the rage.

The best account of how the Michael Jackson coalition of advisers and lawyers and security consultants broke apart can be found in Christopher Andersen's *Michael Jackson: Unauthorized*. The facts are briefly these: Michael's main attorney, Bert Fields, at first had put Anthony Pellicano out front. Pellicano launched his all-out assault to portray 13-year-old Jordie Chandler's father Evan as a wannabe extortionist. Meanwhile, Bert Fields petitioned the court to grant a six-year delay, which, not coincidentally, would be just enough time for the statute of limitations to expire on the criminal charges filed with the court against Michael. The request for a delay was not granted, and we've already seen how Chandler attorney Larry R. Feldman had a public relations field day questioning Michael's self-proclaimed innocence in the face of this obvious and clumsy move to have the statute of limitations expire on the case.

Yet Bert Fields achieved his main objective in filing for the delay. He bought time for the Jackson contingent to formulate their strategy and unify their response. It was during this period that Michael zoomed into Mexico City on October 24. He was increasingly unnerved by the legal moves being made back in L.A. by attorney Feldman on behalf of the Chandlers. So he took more and more drugs. He swallowed Percodan, Demerol and codeine in liberal amounts. He swallowed a raft of tranquilizers, including Valium, Xanax and Ativan.

As previously pointed out, he did not return to the U.S. for the funeral of his mother's father in Phoenix, Arizona, his 100-year-old grandfather Samuel. As

FREAK! Inside the twisted world of Michael Jackson

this funeral took place in Phoenix, seven carloads of police officials turned up at Encino and tossed Hayvenhurst while the family was in Arizona. Michael's mother rushed home to Hayvenhurst in time to get hysterical and call Michael in that condition in Mexico. Michael himself, when he received his mother's call, was teetering on the edge of what mushroomed within hours into a full psychotic break with reality, known more commonly as a nervous breakdown.

But about two weeks before Michael completely flipped out, there was a Jackson contingent summit and strategy meeting in Mexico City. Michael's regular attorney Bert Fields flew down for it, as did Michael's criminal attorney Howard Weitzman. Best friend, surrogate mother, and angel of mercy Liz Taylor also flew down for this all-important conclave. And, most strikingly, Michael's Beverly Hills dermatologist, Arnold Klein flew down. Why a dermatologist, you wonder?

It seems that the Jackson camp had been able to learn that 13-year-old accuser Jordie Chandler had reportedly told the Los Angeles police that Michael Jackson had distinguishing marks on his genitals. Later, reports would state that these distinguishing marks took the form of a tattoo of Winnie the Pooh, as previously mentioned, but the existence of this tattoo was never fully substantiated. What is far more apt is that Michael's genitals were not bleached by acidic agents as the skin on his face, torso, arms and hands had been.

Ever since Michael did his famous long TV interview with Oprah Winfrey in early 1993, he had countered charges that he was trying to bleach himself white by stating that he suffered from vitiligo, a skin disease, as we've seen earlier, that discolors the skin and leaves it blotchy. Michael had told this to Oprah in order to counter the criticism against him that bleaching his skin was an insult to African-Americans. Interestingly, when LaToya's ex-husband and ex-manager Jack Gordon visited agents in the fall of 2002 in New York in an attempt to sell them his version of the Jackson family story, he asserted flatly that Michael did not have a skin disease of any kind, including vitiligo.

According to Gordon, the distinguishing marks on Michael's genitals were their color. They were black, unlike his bleached upper body parts and his face and hands. This would seem to back up the hunch by many at the time of the Mexico City strategy session who speculated that dermatologist Arnold Klein was there to advise the Jackson team. Specifically, skeptics theorized that the dermatologist could have been brought in to tell the Jackson camp just how long it would take to alter or disguise the distinguishing marks on Michael's genitals to negate Jordie Chandler's possible trial testimony.

In his Michael Jackson biography, author Christopher Andersen reported that a top plastic surgeon told him that in six to eight weeks the markings from vitiligo could be changed or even eliminated by employing a combination of ultraviolet light and prescription drugs.

It is easy to see from this why Chandler lawyer Larry R. Feldman pointed out quickly, when it was discovered that Michael Jackson was in the Charter

Nightingale Clinic, that Michael was staying twice to three times as long as the clinic claimed it took to detoxify someone from drugs. Yet, in Michael's defense, six to eight weeks is a short stay by American standards in a rehabilitation center. People in the U.S. often stay three months and sometimes longer, depending on the severity of their addiction. Then again, many recovering pill poppers, alcoholics, potheads and druggies, and any addict caught in a combination thereof in a crossuser bind, might stay in a halfway house for as much as six months to a year after detoxification in a rehab. So there are two sides to this story. It is a valid controversy with feasible explanations on either side.

But, damningly, Michael Jackson did not come off well here. He looked again like the artful dodger, the rich guy hiding behind his resources to avoid facing the music. This perception was reinforced when you learned that both of Michael Jackson's original attorneys, Fields and Weitzman, wanted their client to return to the States immediately and face the charges leveled against him. These two attorneys told Michael correctly that the longer he remained outside the U.S., the guiltier he looked.

All of this infighting got to Bill Bray, the longtime security chief for Michael Jackson who'd been with him since his childhood star days. Bray wanted to bring in star Los Angeles attorney Johnnie L. Cochran. Within eight months, Cochran would become a world famous figure as the lead counsel for football legend Orenthal James Simpson, better known as O.J., in his murder trial for the deaths of his estranged wife Nicole Brown Simpson and her friend Ronald Goldman.

This dissension and infighting in the Michael Jackson camp was adding fuel to the fire and complications to an already jumbled mix. Michael Jackson's manager, Sandy Gallin, had called from Liz Taylor's Bel Air mansion and, along with Liz and Weitzman himself, convinced Michael to appoint Weitzman as his sole spoksperson. Yet now there was pressure on Michael to hire Johnnie Cochran as spokesperson and point man on Micheal's legal team. Liz Taylor objected to this. She was having none of it. She sanely underscored the fact that Michael was in no condition to address such serious issues as which lawyer should represent him.

According to author Andersen, Pellicano told Michael that he would get Michael out of this jam. But a doomsday, "Don't worry, I'll save the day" phone call from Pellicano was the last thing Michael Jackson needed.

When Pellicano told him how bad things were back in California, Michael lit into his advisers and told them that if they didn't fix the situation and fix it fast, he would fire them.

Anthony Pellicano's days as Michael Jackson's security consultant and chief spokesperson on the Chandler case were numbered, and the powwow broke up with Michael insisting he would not return to the States. Instead, he gave his concert performances. He walloped his way into drugs. He had his tooth pulled and was put on more drugs. His mother called hysterical and told him that Hayvenhurst had been tossed by 16 police officials. He called Liz Taylor, who'd returned again to Los

Angeles. On the phone he was weeping and sobbing and threatening suicide. Liz agreed to fly back down immediately and chartered a Learjet for the purpose.

Still, she didn't get there in time.

Before she got there Michael had a massive nervous breakdown, trashed his $5,000-a-night hotel suite, banged his head against the wall, vomited on the rugs, wrote manic "I love you" notes, and scrawled messages on the walls and the furniture.

Until finally he collapsed on the bed in a fetal ball, which is where Liz Taylor found him at one in the morning.

He had lost his mind.

———

November 22 is an ominous day in American history. On a Friday bearing that date 30 years earlier, young, handsome, and vital President John Fitzgerald Kennedy was shot to death as he passed an abandoned book depository in an open Lincoln convertible in Dallas, Texas. Three decades later, while Michael Jackson rested in seclusion in a London rehabilitation center, another bombshell exploded on him eight time zones away in Los Angeles.

Five of his former bodyguards filed a suit against him claiming they had been fired because of what they knew about the superstar's activities with a host of young boys at his Neverland Ranch in Santa Ynez, California, and even earlier at his parents' house in Encino. Here are some of the allegations these five ex-bodyguards made against Michael in their court papers:

■ That he personally ordered one of them to retrieve a Polaroid picture of a naked young boy from his private bathroom and to destroy it.

■ That Michael would sometimes disappear with young boys between the ages of 9 and 14 for long stretches of time, sometimes overnight.

■ That he once had the security personnel keep a young Asian boy in the guardhouse at the front gates of Hayvenhurst until his parents went out for the evening, then had the boy brought to his room.

Bodyguard Leroy Thompson, adding to the details, claimed he was assigned to go to the family house and locate a key hidden under the refrigerator. He said he was then instructed to use the key to enter Michael's private bathroom in his former combination bedroom/playroom. He claimed he was to take a Polaroid that showed a young nude boy that exposed his buttocks and genitals from a side view and see that the photo was destroyed. After he carried out his assignment, Leroy Thompson said Michael Jackson called to confirm with him that he'd done so.

The other four bodyguards who filed the suit were Fred Hammonds, Aaron White, Donald Starks and Morris Williams. All five bodyguards that filed the suit maintained that Michael could not remember which one he'd given the special assignment to destroy the compromising Polaroid. As a simple solution, they stated, Michael Jackson simply had all five of them fired to ensure that the right one was among them.

One week after the five bodyguards filed suit against

Michael Jackson, another story added more bad news for the entertainer, even as he struggled to recover from drug abuse in what for him was not so merry old England. Former chef at the Neverland Ranch, Johnny Ciao, alleged that, while he worked there, he had seen his boss Michael Jackson in compromising circumstances with young boys and with an older artist. Ciao said: "Michael Jackson spent weekends alone in his bedroom and his secret playroom with boys as young as seven — and once I caught him emerging from the playroom naked except for his underwear." Ciao also claimed the following:

■ Michael had a wall in his bedroom walk-in closet covered with about 50 to 60 photos of cute, young boys.

■ Ciao surprised the superstar during an intimate moment with an artist in his 40s visiting from the East Coast. As he walked into the video room, the artist and Michael were seated close together on the floor. Michael moved away from the man, who, obviously disturbed, jumped to his feet and started to redo his undone belt as he rapidly left the room.

■ The angry parents of one young boy came to the house and got into an argument with Michael. Ciao couldn't mollify them with food or drink, as Michael had asked him to, and they left, clearly angry. Upset, Michael retreated to his room that afternoon and did not emerge until the middle of the next day.

Ciao claimed that he kept silent until the five ex-bodyguards filed their suit in Los Angeles on November 22, a few weeks earlier, claiming that Michael had them fired so they couldn't testify against him in court. Ciao also said that never in the eight months he worked for Michael had he ever seen him with a female guest. "But nearly every weekend when Michael was home, there was a young boy staying over alone with him," Ciao said, before adding, "Their ages ranged from seven to fourteen. They were all of a certain type: angelic faces, brown hair and big eyes."

The chef went on to say that the children were brought to the ranch either by their parents or by one of Michael's top aides. He said that the kids would ride up the driveway in a fancy Central Park-style phaeton carriage drawn by a giant Clydesdale. He said the kids were overwhelmed at the sight of the amusement rides and the zoo at Neverland. To the point, this was the same reaction the battle-hardened LAPD veterans had to seeing Neverland for the first time when they showed up with their search warrant in August of '93 while Michael was en route to Bangkok for the start of his Asian leg of the Dangerous tour.

Ciao said the kids stayed over from Friday till Sunday and usually stayed in Michael's bedroom. Ciao had keys to every room in the house, except to Michael's bedroom and the secret playroom. The hallway leading to Michael's bedroom had surveillance equipment that magnified the sound of approaching footsteps.

Also, Ciao stated that the in-house phone in Michael's bedroom only worked for outgoing calls. One couldn't make incoming calls to Michael's bedroom from within the house. Michael always spent time with his young guests in the secret playroom, and he was never to be disturbed while he was in there.

Ciao said that most of the kids came for only one weekend, but that one boy came for five weekends while Ciao worked there. The secret playroom was small and dark and held only a television and an oversize couch, from what Ciao could see. He said Michael also liked to take his young visitors for rides around his ranch on his motorbike. They would sometimes be gone for hours, since the ranch was 2,700 acres.

The chef said he never saw the boys or Michael fully naked, but claimed that once Michael emerged from the secret playroom to pick up a tray of food Ciao had left outside the door. When Ciao glanced back at him, he says he saw that Michael was naked except for a pair of white underpants.

Ciao concluded about all of this: "I never thought at the time that Michael was molesting those boys. I couldn't have stomached working there if I'd even suspected that. Maybe one of the reasons I suspected nothing was because I once asked Michael why he spent so much time with children and he told me with such sincerity: 'Grown-ups are always asking for something. Kids ask for nothing.'

"But after seeing what's happening with him now, I'm very disturbed. What I witnessed was not the behavior of a normal, healthy man. It was all very bizarre and unhealthy."

Michael Jackson's insistence on secrecy and privacy was breaking down rapidly. Attorney Feldman had put pressure on Michael and his team of lawyers to turn over paperwork and to reveal employment records relevant to the six months during which Michael had close contact with his client Jordan Chandler. Feldman was shaking more apples from the tree than he had expected to fall. The contest for the hearts and minds of people in the court of public opinion was swinging heavily in his and his client's favor. Michael Jackson was increasingly enveloped in a bad odor, especially since he refused to disclose to the office of the Los Angeles District Attorney his whereabouts. Since Michael Jackson was not yet charged with a crime, and since no warrant had been issued for his arrest, he was under no strict obligation to tell the Los Angeles district attorney's office where he was. But out of courtesy and in his own public relations interest, he probably should have.

Not only were the Los Angeles authorities looking for Michael in order to interview him, they were also interested in deposing the woman who had run Neverland for years, Norma Staikos. She, too, had vanished and could not be found. She later turned up in her native Greece, specifically in Athens, with her husband. She had not yet been deposed, but she was someone Chandler attorney Feldman very much wanted to hear from. Interestingly, she was named as a defendant in the suit filed on November 22 by the five ex-security guards, as was their other boss, none other than security consultant Anthony Pellicano.

The Jackson camp was running scared — their efforts at counterspin were failing.

Michael was staying out of the country, whether his addiction was real or concocted, an affliction or a scam. He was totally convinced he wanted to remain abroad when the LAPD secured a warrant to have him strip-searched and photographed nude. This development could be viewed as fitting if reports of Michael's photographic activities with his special friends were true.

What was Michael's reaction to his lawyers when they gave him the news he would be strip-searched and photographed?

"Why are they trying to humiliate me?" he cried. "There is no way I am going through that. No way."

But he had spoken, for a change, too soon.

"Michael Jackson Cracks Up — Sex, Drugs and the Fall of the World's Biggest Star." — Headline, People magazine cover story, November 22, 1993.

CHAPTER 9

The very same day that the news hit announcing the lawsuit by Michael Jackson's five ex-bodyguards, People magazine accurately assessed the damage the world's greatest entertainer had done to himself. But Michael, sitting in rehab in London, wasn't too bothered at first. That week, Michael himself was sailing along, figuring he was invulnerable to a real decline, let alone to anything as drastic as a "fall."

MJJ Enterprises was booming. Sales of Michael's records, when the scandal initially broke, took off at first. And that same week Sony announced that the Dangerous album had matched the sales of the Bad album, meaning it had sold 20 million copies also. That meant the combined sales of Michael's last three albums worldwide had topped 80 million units, a staggering number, unmatched by any other artist in the history of the recording industry. Also, that week Michael inked a deal with EMI granting the firm the licensing rights to the ATV Music Publishing Catalog for a term of five years. This was

the catalog of songs that contained nearly all of the
Beatles pop classics, and it was the thorn in Paul
McCartney's side as far as his relationship with
former friend and one-time recording partner
Michael Jackson went. When Michael signed the
deal while still a patient at the Charter Nightingale
Clinic, he received a sign-on payment of
$70 million. So even in rehab Michael was earning a
fortune.

Still, the Pepsi deal, so lucrative for years, was
gone. And though Sony was being cautiously
supportive, other friends in influential positions in
the industry and in society in general were starting to
long-finger Michael. People who clamored to have
their picture taken with him for the past two decades
suddenly were silent and cool. They were not
welcoming and not returning his phone calls.

People like David Geffen, Jacqueline Kennedy
Onassis, Katharine Hepburn, Diana Ross, Liza
Minnelli and hundreds more looked like they were
putting distance between themselves and Michael
Jackson. Hollywood stars were not coming out in
support of Michael as they had at first, when the
Anthony Pellicano "extortion" counteroffensive was
working so well.

It was becoming increasingly clear that Michael's
advisers and his lawyers had not worked as smoothly
and effectively as they hoped. Of course, in their
defense, Michael had steadfastly refused to follow
their counsel and return to the U.S. while the legal
maneuvering was going on through that turbulent
September and October of 1993. By hiding out in
Mexico City and by taking refuge in a rehabilitation

clinic in London that catered to the rich and famous, Michael Jackson had played into the hands of those who said he was countering legal moves with public relations spin. If in fact he was doing that, it didn't matter, because it wasn't working.

When sister LaToya, in her role as Jackson Family Cassandra, held her press conference in Israel on December 8, the rest of the clan gathered the news media outside Hayvenhurst and gave countering statements. As usual, the Jackson family blamed LaToya's actions and pronouncements on her ex-husband and manager, Jack Gordon, who, as stated earlier, had done prison time for attempted bribery charges concerning state gaming officials in Nevada when he owned a brothel there. According to the rest of the Jacksons, Gordon knew how to use his wife to get money out of her and out of her family connections. Michael's oldest brother Jackie characterized Jack Gordon as a "hustler" and his mother Katherine described him as a "mongrel." Mother Katherine also called daughter LaToya a liar. If this Jackson family public relations counteroffensive against LaToya worked on anyone else is a matter of grave indifference because, importantly, it worked on Michael. It scared him into action.

Chandler family lawyer Larry R. Feldman was pushing hard to have Michael Jackson return to the States and finally give his court-ordered deposition on January 18, 1994. Michael had no intention of doing this. So he pressed harder on his legal team to get what he wanted. It was significant that by this time the composition of Michael's legal defense team

had changed, much to Bill Bray and Liz Taylor's
satisfaction. Liz Taylor had joined forces with Bill
Bray in seeing to it that Bert Fields should go. They
wanted him removed and replaced by Johnnie
Cochran. This changing of the legal guard was put in
place in December, when Bert Fields was let go as
well as the man Fields had permitted to lead the
defense to this point — none other than security
consultant Anthony Pellicano.

Johnnie Cochran right from the start had urged
Michael to return home. As he would demonstrate
so well in the case of O.J. Simpson a year later,
Johnnie Cochran knew the power of celebrity, and
he knew as well how difficult it was for a celebrity to
be convicted of a crime if the celebrity met the
charges head-on. Juries were human and were
influenced by close contact with celebrities,
especially if the celebrities played to them like any
other audience.

That's why Cochran wanted Michael to come
home and take the bull by the horns. He
wanted him to turn on the charm and turn the tide
in his favor. But Michael was still hesitant. He still
feared arrest and incarceration. He didn't want the
public spectacle of being arrested, like some common
criminal.

So Cochran and Michael's other legal advisers
negotiated for weeks with the two prosecutors
involved. In Los Angeles they dealt with Gil Garcetti
and in Santa Barbara they dealt with Tom Sneddon.
Finally both of these D.A.'s gave assurances that
Michael would not be met upon his return by
marshals or police detectives wielding handcuffs. If

Michael Jackson set foot on U.S. territory, he would not be faced with a warrant for his arrest or with a court-ordered indictment. Still, Michael resisted. He hesitated until the U.S. prosecutors established contact with the authorities in England. They contacted Scotland Yard with a view to initiating procedures that would have had Michael extradited.

But what really put the fire under Michael was all of the above in combination with his conscientious sister's statements in Israel that she had seen him over the years with as many as 50 to 60 young boys. Her press conference on December 8 alerted Michael that he had to act and act quickly. His sister had potentially opened floodgates that Michael couldn't afford to have open.

He told Johnnie Cochran and his legal team to reach an out-of-court settlement with the Chandlers — and fast. The singer who urged people to open their hearts was going to open his wallet.

But he had no idea how high the price ultimately would be.

━━━━━━━━━

LaToya Jackson's Tel Aviv press conference, in combination with the advice and urging of Johnnie Cochran, also made clear to Michael that he must return to the U.S. So, once again a cloak-and-dagger operation was mounted. This time Michael was extracted from the Charter Nightingale Clinic before dawn and driven in a private ambulance to Heathrow International Airport.

There he boarded a private jet that belonged to one of the world's richest men, the Sultan of Brunei, a friend and fan of Michael's.

The 727 flew to Santa Barbara Airport, making two stops along the way but only to refuel. That early December evening, Michael Jackson emerged from the plane and hopped into a waiting van that sped him to his Neverland Ranch. For companions he had with him again the Cascio brothers, Eddie and Frank.

When Michael got to his ranch, a whole fleet of cars arrived throughout the evening. They contained his lawyers and advisers. Strategy sessions were in order. Christopher Andersen reports in *Michael Jackson: Unauthorized* that one of Michael's advisers was upset to find Michael at Neverland with the two Cascio youngsters. He said to Michael, "Get those two boys out of here, right away!"

Michael didn't take well to this. He informed his critic that if he wanted to remain in Michael's employment, he had to learn to mind his own business. The boys stayed, as they had throughout large segments of the Dangerous tour and they stayed in a very public manner long after the scandal broke and even as it roared toward its crescendo.

Before Michael could in any way get comfortable in Santa Ynez at his ranch, on December 10 the police served him with a warrant for a strip-search. He resisted at first, but his legal advisers told him that the warrant was court mandated and he had to do it. He wept and carried on and swore he wouldn't submit, just as he had said he wouldn't submit to such an indignity when he had first heard of its possibility back in the rehab in London. But he lost this battle.

Ten days later, two detectives showed up at Neverland with an official police department doctor, a still photographer and a video camera operator. Michael protested to the detectives yet again, several times, but to no avail. He eventually stripped and stood naked while his genitals, buttocks and torso were photographed and videotaped from all angles.

There would be much speculation about what the two detectives present, and the police in general, learned from this examination. There is also speculation, never officially confirmed, that the police found a tattoo near Michael's genitals of Winnie the Pooh, of all things.

An associate of Michael's would claim that the strip-search of Michael Jackson's body did not match up with what Jordie Chandler had described. Also, Michael himself would later deny that the police strip-search verified the descriptions of his genitals and midbody given to them by Jordan Chandler.

These denials would hold firm for Michael right down to the present. In the famous interview on television with Diane Sawyer in 1995 with his then wife Lisa Marie Presley, Michael would deny that Jordie Chandler's description of his body was verified by the strip-search and he would deny that police had other evidence against him.

After the strip-search, Michael broke down and wept copiously. He also swore through sobs that his entourage must never let something like that happen again. And he went on the offensive, demanding that his lawyers get the settlement with the Chandlers done and dusted and that they complete this assignment with all due dispatch.

———

When it became clear that a settlement with the Chandlers was just about set, Michael Jackson launched a public relations offensive. He scheduled an address on CNN for December 22, 1993. The address lasted four minutes. He and his team had worked on the wording of what Michael would say in that televised address for two whole days. Before Michael went on the air, he dashed back to his bedroom and put on long false eyelashes, as though he had a date as well as a performance to deliver. He also wore a red shirt and red lipstick and let strands of his hair hang down on either side of his face in a very feminine manner. At the bottom of the TV screen, CNN superimposed a streamer that announced: "Live From Neverland Valley."

Michael started the broadcast by declaring his innocence. Then he said that he would like matters to be resolved quickly. He characterized what he'd been put through as a "horrifying, horrifying experience." He decried the many damaging things written and promulgated about him in the mass media. He requested that everyone "wait to hear the truth before you label or condemn me." He described the strip-search in detail and summed it up as "the most humiliating ordeal of my life . . . a nightmare, a horrifying nightmare." Then he added: "But if this is what I have to endure to prove my innocence, so be it."

At this juncture he reverted to the little boy who'd spent so many hours in Kingdom Hall. He quoted scripture: "If I am guilty of anything, it is of believing what God said about children: 'Suffer little children to come unto me and forbid them not, for such is the Kingdom of Heaven.'" In a startling sentence he then added: "In no way do I think that I am God, but I do try to be God-like in my heart." He ended by invoking his usual blessings from God on everyone and sending everyone his love.

This four-minute televised statement was broadcast all over the world. It appeared, usually in its entirety, on all of that evening's news shows. It also was looped on CNN around the globe.

This wasn't surprising, since the news media had been in a feeding frenzy with this story for four-and-a-half months. And it would remain big news for six more months until another famous celebrity and client of Johnnie Cochran's took over all news, it seemed, when O.J. Simpson drove up and down the L.A. freeways in his white Ford Bronco. As he drove the freeways, Simpson allegedly threatened to kill himself, as he swore he hadn't killed his estranged wife and one of her male friends, Ronald Goldman.

O.J. would eventually avoid criminal prosecution, thanks in large measure to the legal adeptness of one Johnnie Cochran. But O.J. would lose a massive judgment against him in a civil case contending that he was responsible for the two murders in question.

He would also lose his popularity, all of his commercial endorsements, and most of his net worth.

It is safe to speculate that O.J. Simpson also forfeited most of his self-respect, although his denial seemed magnificently strong and unbreachable.

The Juice and Wacko Jacko would come to have more in common than just having the great Johnnie Cochran as a lawyer and advocate.

Jacko had taken big steps toward the ruin of his reputation and of his enormous global following as well. He had also injured himself financially. He had likewise lost his endorsements. He had, in addition, wrecked many of his important contacts and friendships. Jacko and Juice were birds of a feather. They were rich guys who got over in terms of real or potential criminal prosecution.

But neither would get off and go scot-free in the court of public opinion.

Just as the Juice would annihilate himself eventually in a proceeding in civil court, Jacko had self-imploded as well. Each had courted disaster.

And each would suffer enormous damage, a kind of self-ruination.

"Don't treat me like a criminal, because I am innocent." — Michael Jackson in a live telecast on CNN on December 22, 1993.

CHAPTER 10

Michael Jackson thought he'd saved the day. He thought that by going on CNN and taking his case to the public he would vanquish anyone with the audacity to take him on. Over the weeks following the CNN telecast, he was often seen out in public. He even made public appearances and gave speeches at industry functions at which he declared his utter innocence of the child molestation charges and received standing ovations in return. He went in and out of Vegas, as he used to do, and he felt he'd come out of this Jordie Chandler mishap smelling like the proverbial rose.

He was wrong.

He had indeed kick-started the process that would lead to an out-of-court settlement with the Chandlers, but he had again underestimated the resolve of both the Chandlers and their lawyer, the redoubtable Larry R. Feldman.

They had at the beginning of this scandal refused to be plowed under by Anthony Pellicano, and now they wanted the settlement they sought, not just the one Michael Jackson and his team of lawyers and advisers wanted to allow them.

There have been various reports about the settlement Michael Jackson paid to the Chandlers, with figures running from that initially ludicrous $375,000 offer advanced in the early days of the crisis by Anthony Pellicano to the gargantuan reports of a settlement of $40 million.

Christopher Andersen reported in *Michael Jackson: Unathorized,* that Michael Jackson paid the Chandlers the sum of $26 million. According to Andersen, one million went to Evan Chandler and the remaining $25 million was to be paid in five annual installments of $5 million each into a trust fund overseen for Jordan Chandler, under the prudent man rules, by a retired judge.

Michael Jackson would later tell his friends Donald and Marla Trump that the amount he paid the Chandlers was "peanuts," but no normal person with a normal income would view $26 million as peanuts. Michael's team tried to minimize the amount in order to cast the whole crisis in the minor category of a nuisance suit. This whole Chandler affair was certainly far more than a nuisance suit and Michael would shortly learn how far reaching and devastating the consequences would be.

The whole deal was a whitewash by Michael Jackson and his team. Especially since Michael had been back in the States, they had felt the walls closing in and the heat coming down on them. The Santa Barbara D.A.'s office had subpoenaed lawyer Larry R. Feldman's files on the case for use in a potential criminal court case against Michael Jackson.

In Santa Barbara, which is the county seat right near Santa Ynez and Neverland, officials had started to convene a grand jury to question witnesses in connection with the molestation charges against Michael Jackson. Police were also gathering new evidence in the civil case that they could use in the potential criminal cases.

Attorney Feldman was pushing to have more and more acquaintances and former employees of Michael Jackson deposed for possible court use. This included such people as Michael's outspoken sister LaToya and his former bodyguard, Miko Brando, Marlon's son. There was talk, as well, of deposing Marlon Brando himself, since the renowned actor served as a kind of father surrogate for Michael, much as Liz Taylor functioned as a surrogate mother.

Chandler attorney Feldman was pressing hard also for the names and dates of employment of maids, cooks, secretaries, and even road managers who'd worked on Michael's various world tours promoting his albums.

Feldman delivered an even more crippling blow by petitioning the courts to allow him and his clients access to the photographs and videos taken of Michael's genitals, buttocks, midsection and torso during the police strip-search on December 20. Then Feldman cleverly knocked the Jackson camp for another loop by filing a motion with the court to have Michael Jackson reveal his net worth. Feldman must have known that this information about Michael's personal finances would leak to the press and compromise the superstar's privacy deeply.

All told, the Jackson camp knew they were surrounded and being backed into a very narrow corner. Michael Jackson could play hardball in business with the best of them. He was a shrewd and brilliant negotiator. He had demonstrated his smarts as an entertainer and as a businessman from an early age. He had had the guts to fire his own father, to drive legendarily canny business deals to their conclusion to his advantage, to fire anyone who, in his view, didn't deliver for him.

Yet he knew not to play hardball with Feldman and Evan Chandler.

After the settlement in the Chandler affair was announced, the prosecutors in Los Angeles and in Santa Barbara were left holding the empty legal bag. Without a "victim willing to testify," it is very difficult to press a criminal case where the alleged crime is sexual molestation.

So after Michael Jackson settled with the Chandlers out of court in the civil court action, the question of criminal prosecution was derailed because Jordie Chandler was no longer willing to testify in criminal court against Michael Jackson.

Michael's people were claiming that Michael had virtually been entrapped and framed by the

Chandlers. Of course, anyone would wonder why parents would allow their young and adolescent male children to comport themselves regularly with a man 20- or 30-odd years their senior in the first place. It is a valid point of skepticism.

Michael raves about children and their innocence and honesty and directness. Par for the course. Their enthusiasms thrill him. They need his love and care. Of course, they do. And many pedophiles build elaborate playgrounds and play rooms. They build shrines of dolls and big boxes full of toys. They build big and elaborate dollhouses and construct huge and realistic sets of toy trains and so on.

All of these are mere seduction tools. They all blend perfectly with the MO of a pedophile. For sure, not every pedophile has the resources of a Michael Jackson, so not all of them can build their own amusement park and zoo and entertain children for hours and dazzle their eyes out of their heads while doing it.

But if you do have the resources of a Michael Jackson and do build something like the Neverland Ranch, of course the kids will love it.

Just as they'll love shopping sprees when they're the center of attention and their every wish is the Daddy Warbucks-like pedophile's command.

But Michael Jackson's campaign to rehabilitate his image and make him out to be an innocent man was counterred by plenty of circumstantial evidence against Michael.

The Chandler affair and its potential criminal

charges against Michael Jackson just got derailed when he, so to speak, bought the railroad and retired the little engine that could!

In 1994, it was reported that Michael Jackson forgave his sister LaToya for speaking out against him in her press conference in Tel Aviv on December 8, 1993. Michael forgave her "betrayal.

"Well, I was sad about it," Michael was reported as saying. "But she is my sister, and throughout this whole thing I vowed to never hate anyone involved, but rather bless them. So, bless you, LaToya."

It is always smart to take the high road in disputes and in ugly situations, but it never works if you do it too late. Michael Jackson was easily a day late and a dollar short.

Michael Jackson's gambit here was to cast himself as the high-minded Christ-like forgiver of stained human nature. Even so, Michael Jackson's pal Elton John was quoted as saying: "I wouldn't have settled. I wouldn't have cared if I had to sell the last thing in my life just to clear my name."

Like lots of Michael Jackson's celebrity friends, and like lots of ordinary people, Elton John clearly thinks that the Michael Jackson pay-off to the Chandlers was a mistake.

On January 25, 1994, attorneys Johnnie Cochran and Larry R. Feldman jointly announced a settlement in the Chandler affair outside the Santa Monica courthouse in Los Angeles. The day before, the district attorney's office had cleared Evan Chandler of any charges of extortion. The D.A.'s office said that they could find no evidence of any such behavior on the part of Evan Chandler.

In this joint press conference with Johnnie Cochran, Larry Feldman stated that Michael Jackson maintained his innocence but had dropped all allegations of extortion. He said that the matter between the Chandlers and Michael Jackson was now settled. He said that the parties involved could now put this matter behind them and get on with their lives. He concluded his remarks by stating that Jordan Chandler himself, referred to only as "the boy," was happy that the matter had been resolved.

Johnnie Cochran then told the assembled reporters and media crews: "Michael Jackson is an innocent man." He paused and added, "The time has come for Michael Jackson to get on with his life."

Not many people, at the end of the day, would agree, in the court of public opinion, that Michael Jackson was an innocent man. And the life Michael Jackson was to get on with was permanently and irreparably damaged. He had toppled himself from the pinnacle. He would no longer be the world's most famous entertainer. He would no longer be viewed as a freak in the sense of someone extraordinarily gifted.

No, he would spend all of his life, from here on out, in moves calculated to dispel the impression that he was a freak in the negative sense of the world, that of a weirdo and a creep.

"Having been accused of child molestation, he's obviously wanting to create a new image of a happily married man." — Judge Hugo Francisco Alvarez, two months after he presided over the Jackson-Presley marriage ceremony.

CHAPTER 11

Right from the time Michael Jackson settled the Chandler affair with a multimillion-dollar payoff, he had a huge public relations problem on his hands. People do not believe someone is innocent who is willing to buy another person's silence. Nor do they believe someone is innocent who is afraid to confront an accuser in court and turn that accuser away, an empty-handed loser red-faced with embarrassment. Because Michael Jackson settled with the Chandlers, the perception of him on the street among many people is that he is a compulsive pedophile, a sexual addict in a way that most people find repellent. People these days often turn up their noses at the mention of his name. He is reviled by many and seen as decadent and deeply troubled.

On May 26, 1994, Michael Jackson married Lisa Marie Presley, the daughter of the King of Rock 'n' Roll himself, Elvis Presley. They were married in a secret ceremony in the Dominican Republic. Even the ceremony was bizarre. Newspapers around the world had a field day describing how casually dressed the bride groom was and how cavalierly he responded to the judge's question, "Do you take this woman, Lisa Marie Presley, to be your lawfully wedded wife?"

According to sources, Jacko flippantly replied, "Why not?"

It's the little things that always give you away, and this response shows exactly where the Gloved One's head was at the time. He didn't take his own marriage seriously and neither did anyone else with an IQ in double digits. This move was clearly the old wedding bells as the ultimate sexual bearding trick, and of course it didn't work.

"Michael looked like a little boy lost," said Judge Hugo Francisco Alvarez, who presided over the ceremony. "He stared at the floor throughout the ceremony — and when I pronounced him and Lisa Marie man and wife, he was reluctant to kiss her."

The judge went on to describe other aspects of the wedding that were unusual: "There were no tears of happiness, no joy, no laughter. The ceremony had a somber tone. It was bizarre." Judge Alvarez said that Michael Jackson, a perpetual Peter Pan fan, originally wanted to be married up in the air, while flying around. He wanted the judge to perform the ceremony while Michael's private plane circled the island. But this kooky request the judge could not honor, as he explained to Michael's representatives. His authority to marry people was only valid on the soil of the Dominican Republic. If the wedding had been performed in an airborne plane, it would have been invalid.

So Michael Jackson and Lisa Marie Presley went to

the judge's private home in La Vega on May 26th and there the couple was married. During the ceremony both Michael and Lisa Marie wore dark glasses and black hats similar to those worn by flamenco dancers. Michael was his usual cuckoo self. He was more fascinated with the tie Judge Alvarez wore than he was interested in anything else, including his new bride. Of course, the tie showed a cartoon character, Fred Flintstone. The judge had bought the tie at Universal Studios in Florida. He said that Michael told him: "It's a great tie — I love Fred Flintstone!"

Then the judge added: "But I never heard him say he loved Lisa Marie."

Consider another unusual note to this whole nuptial proceeding, so to speak. You would think that a wedding ceremony between two people so linked with musical fame would include some music — but, no, there was none. The entire ceremony was performed in stony silence. Here's the clincher: Michael and Lisa Marie didn't sleep together while they were in the Dominican Republic. They slept in separate beds — in separate houses even. Michael slept in a $4 million oceanfront home that belonged to the owners of the Casa de Campo resort, while Lisa Marie stayed in Villa 11, five miles away from Michael.

Insiders say the whole marriage was a sham, but Michael Jackson and his public relations juggernaut tried really hard at first to make everything look real and on the level.

But not all the king's horses or all the king's men could put Michael Jackson back together again. He had broken basic taboos of behavior in American culture. He and his advisers had pursued a colossally damaging course of action in the Chandler affair.

The world had not yet invented fire control and damage control systems that could handle, let alone repair or restore, the injury to his image Michael Jackson had done.

He had set his feet on the tawny and stained yellow brick road that would lead him from being the world's most famous entertainer to the world's most notorious freak.

And there wasn't a Band-Aid or a cosmetic or a plastic surgeon's scalpel in the entire world big enough to cover, let alone repair or heal, the wound Michael Jackson had inflicted on himself.

———

That is not to say that the Michael Jackson public relations juggernaut wouldn't try to re-create Michael Jackson megastar in the light they wanted him to be perceived. In a world exclusive interview and photo session, the National Enquirer published an eight-page spread in the August 23, 1994 issue. Michael Jackson and Lisa Marie Presley were ostensibly at that time on their honeymoon in New York City. They were staying in their Trump Tower penthouse apartment, and they invited top celebrity photographer Dick Zimmerman to join them there and photograph them for the entire world to see.

The marriage, at first kept secret, was now to be publicized across the known universe. Just one day before the photo session, Lisa Marie had announced to the assembled press that she and Michael Jackson were indeed man and wife.

Dick Zimmerman was the same photographer who snapped the shots of Michael used on Thriller — the front cover and the inside spread. It's unimaginable from the perspective of today that a man as good-looking as Michael Jackson then was would have had his looks altered by plastic surgery even more, to the degree where he became the disfigured freak he is at present. Not incidentally, in the Thriller photos he is still clearly a black man — an unbelievably attractive black man — so what was the reason for all the alterations? What was the problem?

In the article accompanying the photos in the Enquirer, photographer Zimmerman had this to say: "This couple is madly in love! It's a real marriage, not a hoax. Lisa Marie has two children and they're going to be part of a normal family with her and Michael." He explained how he came to have the assignment to officially photograph the happy couple. "Lisa's secretary called me and then Lisa got on the phone. She just told me, 'You're the one. We'd like you to do it.' " There was a whole clutch of photographers from all over the world camped outside Trump Tower, hoping to get a quick shot of Michael and Lisa Marie, but Zimmerman landed the official assignment.

In the article, Zimmerman told how the photoshoot came about: "On August 2, I smuggled photographic equipment into the Trump Tower right under the eyes of the paparazzi outside. Michael and

Lisa Marie were waiting to greet me. While I was setting up my equipment in their living room, Lisa Marie and Michael were being made up by makeup artists hired for the occasion. I left the choice of clothes to them. Michael selected a black military-style jacket with gold leaf embroidery and tassels. His makeup made him look very light-skinned. Lisa Marie wore black pants and a matching long black jacket.

"For the first shot, I told them to stand close to each other and relax. They immediately put their arms around each other and Lisa Marie cuddled right up to Michael. Then I told them to change into casual outfits. Michael chose a red military-style shirt with a blue-striped collar. Lisa Marie changed into a white blouse, black jacket and blue jeans with the knees out. They both had their makeup touched up.

"For the second photo, Michael sat on the floor. Lisa Marie put her arm around his neck and nestled her face lovingly into his hair. Michael broke into a beautiful, spontaneous smile. Then I told Lisa Marie to sit in a chair and Michael to kneel beside her. He put his arm around her and pulled her head into his chest, while Lisa Marie tenderly took hold of his hand. Between shots, they were whispering and giggling to each other, enjoying little jokes."

Eventually during the photo session Zimmerman decided he wanted to set up for an "artistic mood shot, with light and shade." So he told Michael and for Lisa Marie "to put their heads together and Lisa Marie to put both her arms around Michael, hugging him tight. Normally a photographer has to manipulate people into what he wants. But in this case, they were so happy and natural it was almost difficult to keep their attention on the camera. They were so much into each other."

In an inset in the eight-page spread, there was a close-up of Lisa Marie's hand with an enormous diamond and gold ring on it, her wedding ring. In some of the shots Zimmerman took, Lisa Marie wore the ring on her left hand. In other shots she wore it on her right hand. Said Zimmerman: "That was never explained to me. All I know is that Lisa wanted to show off her wedding ring."

The celebrated photographer did elaborate about how he viewed the new married couple and their relationship: "Clearly they wanted to show off to the world how happy they are with each other. They didn't put it into words for me. They didn't have to. The pictures show it."

There were rumors around that Lisa Marie was pregnant by Michael. And Zimmerman added: "They didn't say anything to me about it. But I'd be very happy for them if Lisa was pregnant. And I'd be delighted to take the baby pictures!"

In the photos, Michael and Lisa Marie are draped all over each other, but Michael's eyes are always focused on the camera. He plays exclusively to the lens. He touches Lisa Marie when they're draped all over each other, but he does it lightly and tentatively. She, on the other hand, is obviously into it. She touches Michael with real enthusiasm. She throws herself toward him. He merely leans into her, holding back, watching the camera.

This is Michael Jackson hard at work to prove that

he is "a regular guy." Remember, that is how he described himself to the visiting publishers in August of 2002, when he pitched them his new book in Stamford, Connecticut, the book that was going to set the record straight. It's hard to imagine this photo-spread-cum-news-article, staged publicity stunt fooling anyone.

But you can't blame Michael and his camp for trying. It's just that, for anyone capable of insight and sophistication, this whole spin campaign cum sideshow really was like watching an infant trying to put a marshmallow in a piggy bank.

A month after the eight-page lovey-dovey photo spread appeared in the National Enquirer, Michael Jackson stated that he had had his eye on pretty little Lisa Marie since she was 5 years old. That was when he first met her, when he and his brothers visited her dad Elvis in Lake Tahoe in 1973.

The Jackson brothers had been with Motown only a short while then, and Berry Gordy sent them to Tahoe to take in the King's act and possibly pick up pointers from him. As Michael explained: "I was there to see Elvis perform. We had just signed with Motown, who sent us there to see The King to get some tips. And Lisa Marie was backstage. She was a cute little kid."

This explains how Michael and Lisa Marie became friends and kept in touch over the years. Then they met up six months before they got married, when

Michael approached Lisa Marie for permission to record one of Elvis's songs for his upcoming album tilted Family History. Before long, the two were taking Lisa Marie's two kids, Danielle, 5, and Benjamin, 2, to Disneyland. Michaelfollowed this up with invitations for all three to visit him at the Neverland Valley Ranch. They did this several times. Oddly enough, Michael said that he started to fall in love with Lisa Marie because she was wonderful with his animals. Michael said, "One of the things that most attracted me to Lisa is that she gets along well with the many animals in my zoo."

Things between these lovebirds apparently heated up when they spent a week at Donald Trump's place in Palm Beach, Florida. Next, after the happy couple returned to California, before anyone knew what was happening, Lisa Marie was parading up the stairs at Neverland in a bathrobe. And, wouldn't you know it, here came Michael down those same stairs a while later wearing his Mickey Mouse pajamas and sporting a big grin on his face, a version of Don Juan decked out in kiddie pj's. From then on, according to an inside source at the ranch, the two were practically inseparable.

Michael also disclosed how he came to propose to Lisa Marie. Here is his account of the proposal in his own words: "Lisa Marie and I were in the living room having a glass of wine. We had just finished watching All About Eve, starring Bette Davis. We both love that movie. I just walked over to her, reached into my pocket and pulled out a huge diamond ring. 'So, what do you think?' I asked her. 'You wanna?' I never even officially popped the question. We never actually discussed marriage. It just sort of happened."

Of a prenuptial agreement, Michael said: "I would never ask Lisa Marie to sign a prenuptial agreement. What kind of marriage would that be? C'mon, no one marries anyone for money."

This is a naive statement on Michael's part. Plenty of people marry for money every day. But it probably was not the case with him and Lisa Marie. At the time he was estimated to be worth just an eyelash under half a billion dollars. Lisa Marie then was worth about $9 million. But in a matter of a few years she was slated to come into another sum estimated somewhere between $80 and $200 million. This would happen when she came to control her late father's estate, which her mother Priscilla had cleverly and spectacularly enhanced in value over the years since Elvis's death in 1977, when Lisa Marie was only 9 years old.

Michael went on to explain the nature of his relationship to Lisa Marie, now that they were married: "This is love. I swear it. I love Lisa Marie. Why won't people believe that? Why won't the public let me be happy? I don't get it."

He said that he understood that some of the problems people had in believing his marriage to Lisa Marie was real stemmed from his strange behavior at the wedding ceremony in the Dominican Republic. He explained that he was merely nervous at their wedding ceremony, and that he never meant to be disrespectful. It was unfortunate that a lot of people perceived him as being nonchalant and dismissive about something as serious as being married.

Later, Michael addressed the subject of having children. "Yes, we want to have children," he added. "Yes, we will have children. But, no, she in not expecting right now. Don't rush me."

Michael and Lisa Marie had made the front pages of newspapers around the world when he kissed her right on stage at the MTV Awards show in Manhattan. If that wasn't proof enough of the validity of their marriage, Michael didn't know what to do to convince skeptics.

"Really, this is not a hoax," he concluded. "I swear it's not. And I don't care what people think. I really don't. All I want people to know is that I wouldn't marry someone just for publicity. That's just not me. I love her. This is serious. I hope people believe it. If not, then hey, too bad for them."

Either Michael was delusional or just plain silly. His marriage would be in trouble shortly and it would prove to be short-lived. Over the next few months, articles appeared that showed Michael and Lisa Marie as lovebirds. Other articles turned up saying Michael wanted to move into Graceland and that he wanted to perform in some of Elvis's old outfits, altered, of course, to fit him.

A few articles pointed out that Priscilla was not crazy about her new son-in-law. She was said to have been angered when informed that only daughter and heir Lisa Marie had married Michael. Oddly, though, Michael said that he didn't have Lisa Marie sign a prenuptial agreement. Later articles claimed that Priscilla, shortly after being informed of the marriage, insisted that Michael and Lisa Marie sign a binding agreement forever keeping their respective fortunes separate. The Neverland fortune and the Graceland fortune were thereby assured of remaining in only one person's hands, Neverland in Michael's and Graceland's in Lisa Marie's.

But the public was not convinced by all of the spin Michael Jackson was putting on his life as husband and stepfather and ardent lover of Lisa Marie Presley.

Far from it.

Jokes abounded about the marriage. The late-night TV comedy shows continued to draw rich material on Michael Jackson, as they had since the '70s and '80s, when Joan Rivers especially never lost an opportunity to make sport of Michael Jackson and to mock him roundly.

One cartoon that appeared in print said it all. In the background of this cartoon, Michael, in his signature black fedora and sunglasses, is standing naked in the doorway to his and Lisa Marie's bedroom. In the foreground, Lisa Marie sits naked on their bed, her leg crooked so that it discreetly covers Michael's groin from the viewer's gaze as he stands in the doorway in the distance. A dialogue bubble over Lisa's head says: "So that's where you keep your other glove."

A cartoon is a small thing, but somehow this cartoon makes a big statement. And that statement is simply that the public was not buying into the new, re-created Michael Jackson. Michael Jackson — the married man — was not making it as a new public image.

On Flag Day, June 14, 1995, Diane Sawyer interviewed Michael Jackson and Lisa Marie Presley on ABC's Primetime Live. More than 60 million people watched the interview. Evan Chandler, the Beverly Hills dentist and father of Jordan Chandler, later sued Michael Jackson, ABC, and Diane Sawyer over the content of this broadcast. Jordan Chandler is, of course, the then 13-year-old boy who sued Michael Jackson for sexual molestation in 1993. Evan Chandler felt that the show was a whitewash on behalf of Michael Jackson.

Evan Chandler maintained that Michael Jackson was allowed to promulgate lies on the show because Diane Sawyer was journalistically negligent in her responsibilities to point out falsehoods laid out by Jackson in this interview that she knew to be untrue. Diane Sawyer was taken to court by Evan Chandler. What's more, she was also taken to task by other journalists, who criticized her performance. These critics felt that she had let Michael Jackson use her as a public relations flack who was afraid to challenge him, the way a tougher and more trenchant journalist would have.

Vanity Fair subsequently ran an article on the interview showing how Diane Sawyer had let statements go unchallenged by Michael Jackson that should have been countered by facts and evidence.

Two months after the Primetime Live interview ran on TV, D.A. Insiders say Sneddon told Vanity Fair that Michael Jackson had lied during the TV show when he said that there were no identifying marks on his genitals to link him to the accusations of sexual abuse made against him by young Jordan

Chandler. Said D.A. Sneddon: "His statement on TV is untrue and incorrect and not consistent with the   evidence   in this case."

Tom Sneddon went on to state that Michael Jackson had pretty much told Diane Sawyer a fairy tale when he stated that police had not found incriminating evidence against him in their searches of his various residences. Said Sneddon: "The idea that there are not any photos or pictures or anything is pure poppycock. In the search, Jackson said they didn't find anything unless it was 'something somebody sent me.' That is not true."

The Vanity Fair article quoted sources that alleged the police had found a book of naked young boys at play — something that was often found in the possession of pedophiles. The article also claimed that the police confiscated for evidence a picture of a naked young boy wrapped in a sheet in Michael's bedroom.

The worst aspect of Diane Sawyer's interview, in the view of D.A. Sneddon, was that she got the facts in the case completely wrong. She announced that Jackson had been "cleared of all the charges — we want to make that clear." Not so, according to Sneddon. He stated: "Michael Jackson has not been cleared. The state of the investigation is in suspension until somebody comes forward."

Dr. Doe Lang, a psychologist who had taught communications skills at the New School in Manhattan, commented on the body language used by Michael Jackson and by Lisa Marie Presley while they were on camera. Dr. Lang is a well-known expert on body language. She noted that Michael Jackson took every opportunity to distance himself during the interview, though Lisa Marie was just the opposite, trying at all times to unite them. Michael also constantly used the pronoun "I" instead of "we." What's more, Michael's body language established that he was definitely the boss in their marriage, and that Lisa Marie took a submissive role toward him. Dr. Lang noted that Michael displayed an attitude that said he was pretty much the king, to be obeyed and venerated. Lisa Marie got very little consideration from him as his wife. She acted as if she was totally in awe of him.

It is interesting to note that Diane Sawyer displeased Michael Jackson during this now famous interview. Although some people thought she was soft on him, he did not feel this way. He felt that she was far too hard on him throughout the interview. This is the reason he was still complaining about her and the interview as late as August of 2002, when he interviewed prospective publishers trying to induce them to buy his latest book, the book destined to set the record straight, according to him.

It was clear to the visiting publishers in August 2002, that by "setting the record straight" Michael Jackson meant something more along the lines of The World According to Michael Jackson.

Ever and again, it is crystal clear that Michael Jackson is in denial to the point of self-delusion and beyond. Because he believes nonsense and denies reality he convinces himself that he can induce others to join him in this sorry state of mental fantasy.

It doesn't work. The public has ceased to see

Michael Jackson the way he wants to be seen. And no trick mirrors or fun house gambits are going to change this fact. Michael Jackson had ruined his image and damaged his career and nothing was ever going to set it straight. Especially not a flaky marriage that was about to fall apart.

———

Right after the interview with Diane Sawyer, everything for Michael Jackson and Lisa Marie Presley seemed rosy. In newspaper articles they proclaimed their happiness, and the joy of their sex life together, and how Lisa Marie was now poised and ready to fulfill her aspirations as an actress, and how they planned to have children.

But trouble loomed and lurked on the horizon.

Two months later, the story broke that Michael and Lisa Marie were having a serious row over Macaulay Culkin, one of Michael's special friends. It seems that Michael was prepared to build a new house for Macaulay on the grounds of the Neverland Ranch. Michael devoted nearly all of his time to helping his friend Macaulay. Lisa Marie felt ignored. She was quoted as fuming that her husband "seems to think that that little brat needs him more than his own wife." It was further revealed that Lisa Marie and Michael did not sleep in the same room because she could not tolerate his snoring. She also could not abide the way he played mind games. She particularly resented the way he'd say they were going out for a ride and then she'd find herself at the airport jetting off to some distant place with him.

There had been reports of Michael and Lisa Marie starting to quarrel. They had an especially bad argument over Michael's temper tantrum reaction when Lisa Marie's son Benjamin pulled Michael's new wig off while the two were horsing around at the Santa Ynez ranch. After this fracas, Michael flew off in a snit to sulk in France while Lisa Marie languished alone 7,000 miles away.

Strains were showing up in this fairytale marriage but fast. No more than four months later, Michael Jackson was squiring the Cascio brothers again. These were the two young brothers from New Jersey that Michael had spent so much time palling around with on the ill-fated Dangerous tour. He had flaunted his relationship with these brothers in late summer and all through the fall of 1993, even in the teeth of the Chandler affair and its concomitant scandal.

In December the two brothers, Frank, now 15, and Eddie, now 11, were reportedly set to spend Christmas at the Neverland Ranch with Michael, who was showering the boys with gifts and dressing them in expensive designer outfits. The Cascio family had also received lots of benefits from the two sons hanging out with Michael Jackson.

Their father had gone from working at the Helmsley Palace Hotel, where he first met Michael Jackson and introduced him to his handsome sons, to owning two restaurants. In addition, the Cascio family had moved from a small bungalow in a shabby neighborhood to a five-bedroom hilltop house in an upscale section of Franklin Lakes, New Jersey. This new house even had a swimming pool and a tennis court.

According to the Cascio's neighbors, Michael Jackson would suddenly show up and sweep the boys into a limousine and take them on trips or to Neverland. These same neighbors testified that Michael Jackson was interfering with the boys' natural friendships with kids their own age. Said one neighbor: "I think it's really very selfish of Michael to take two young boys out of their neighborhood, away from their friends of the same age, just so he'll have someone to keep him company."

Then, right after Christmas, Michael collapsed at the Beacon Theater on Manhattan's West Side while rehearsing for a comeback concert. He spent six days in the intensive care unit at New York's Beth Israel North Medical Center.

While he was in the hospital Lisa Marie stayed at his bedside. But as soon as doctors released Michael, he flew off to Paris and proceeded straight to Euro-Disney, where he ensconced himself in the $500-a-night Sleeping Beauty Suite at the Disney Hotel. He then played for days with French children, while ignoring his own stepchildren back at home with Lisa Marie.

It came as a surprise to no one capable of whistling and walking at the same time that Lisa Marie filed for divorce from Michael Joe Jackson early in the new year of 1996.

━━━━━━━━━

Within weeks of the announcement on January 18, 1996, that Lisa Marie Presley was suing Michael

Jackson for divorce, articles appeared that reported — surprise, surprise — that their marriage had been a sham right from the start. The following allegations about Michael Jackson and his recent marriage surfaced:

■ Michael left out lingerie in his bedroom to make it look like he and Lisa Marie were sleeping together.

■ He bugged Lisa Marie's room and monitored her phone calls.

■ He doted on his young male pals and gave Lisa Marie short shrift.

■ He never even slept, or shared a bedroom, with his wife.

These claims were allegedly based on the testimony of five former staff members at Neverland. A maid, three security guards and an office worker had filed a suit against Michael the previous February claiming that he had bugged their quarters and spied on them. Therefore, they claimed, he had violated their civil rights. There had been earlier reports that Neverland was loaded with spying and eavesdropping equipment, and that Michael had used it on guests, including his dear friend and surrogate mother Elizabeth Taylor.

This disclosure was quickly followed by others asserting that the Jackson-Presley divorce could very well end up being among Hollywood's most complex and costly. Yet one article held that Lisa Marie had filed for divorce at her mother Priscilla's encouragement because Lisa Marie was due to come into her inheritance from her father Elvis's estate and she should take a dramatic step to protect her new assets from her husband.

Before you could whisper the phrase "confidentiality agreement," another ex-bodyguard of Michael's filed suit against him in Los Angeles Superior Court. The man who filed the suit was Jerome Johnson, and he asserted that he was fired after he complained about his colleagues having to lie on behalf of Michael Jackson to help him dispel charges against him of child molestation.

The suit also held that Michael Jackson's drug dependency was only a ploy to stay abroad while avoiding the authorities in the U.S. looking into the charges. Mr. Johnson also stated that Michael Jackson frequently had young boys spend the night with him while he was on the Dangerous tour. And, even after Mr. Johnson was fired, he said that lawyers for Michael Jackson tried to pressure him to sign a document full of lies to protect the superstar from the grand jury investigation underway in Santa Barbara.

There were also reports on the divorce that alleged that Michael Jackson's income had fallen sharply. Sales of his HIStory album in 1995 tumbled from the Top 20 within two months. His collapse a few weeks before Lisa Marie filed for divorce had placed Michael's projected tour to promote the HIStory album in jeopardy.

So the great big experiment in spin control following the Chandler affair catastrophe had ended in ruin.

What Michael Jackson could not get through his surgically much-worked-on head was this simple truth: He had covered himself in shame and there would be no resurrection.

"Michael Jackson is calculating and ruthless. The marriage was a terrible mistake." — Lisa Marie Presley to a friend, March 26, 1996.

CHAPTER 12

Michael Jackson was not through trying to change his image. He managed to work out a divorce settlement with Lisa Marie Presley that paid her, according to reports, a settlement of $15 million.

This settlement, if true, ensured her friendship and her continued silence about their relationship and marriage, and especially about Michael's involvement with young boys all the while they were together.

Lisa Marie told a pal that her feelings about her marriage to Michael Jackson really amounted to a sense of having brought shame on herself and her family name. "I feel deeply guilty about it. I brought shame on my father. I suppose that is why I am having awful dreams."

A friend said that Lisa had gone back to the Church of Scientology in search of comfort. She had belonged to the Church of Scientology before she married Michael, and she had even induced him to accompany her to functions at the community center run by the Church of Scientology. Her friend had this to say about Lisa Marie and what shape her mind was in over the separation and impending divorce: "If she wasn't a Scientologist, she'd be going to a psychologist for therapy. But we don't believe in psychiatrists or psychologists. We get better results with what we call auditing. It's a procedure designed to clear the mind of past troubles, past hang-ups."

The friend said that this technique of auditing was designed to "rid her [Lisa Marie] of the anger she feels about the marriage to Michael Jackson. And they are trying to relieve her of her awful nightmares. The dream that most haunts her revolves around Elvis. He comes to her as a handsome young man and bends down to give her a kiss. Just as his lips touch her cheek he turns into an ugly, bloated corpse. Lisa Marie wakes up screaming, saying, 'He's angry, he hates me! I knew he would never have approved of my marriage to Michael. Now I can only pray he will forgive me.'"

It was obvious that Michael Jackson was fully capable of using people in a cruel and calculated manner to get what he wanted, no matter the price to the victims he exploited. This belies the image he promotes of himself as a sensitive and caring humanitarian at all times. His capacity for cruelty to women seems large, to put it diplomatically. Lisa Marie Presley was a needy little rich girl he exploited from A to Z. It even infuriated Lisa Marie's ex-husband Danny Keough, a rock musician and the father of her two children. Pals say he told them: "The thought of Lisa Marie as Michael Jackson's wife was revolting to me. There were nights when I couldn't sleep thinking she was with that weird man. Worse, my children were with him. That was the cruelest blow of all."

No one can doubt that Michael Jackson messed with Lisa Marie's mind. There had been rumors right from the start of their marriage that Jacko was running an embellished publicity scam with the whole affair. There were also whispers that Jackson had enticed Lisa Marie with promises of support from him in her dream of being an entertainer, like her famous father, and an actress, as her mother Priscilla had been before she married Elvis and gave birth to Lisa Marie. In other words, Michael Jackson strung her along, raised her hopes and expectations, then dropped her like a stone as soon as he could resume his games with his special friends, the young boys he so favored.

It was reported that ex-husband Danny was still in love with Lisa Marie, but that he didn't want to discuss remarriage with her until she had sorted herself out from this Michael Jackson fiasco and settled down. She was further described as unable to decide whether in life she wanted to be a mother and wife or a rock star. She was so up in the air and discombobulated with everything that she had even let her mother Priscilla continue to handle the Elvis Presley estate, even though Lisa Marie was now old enough and legally entitled to manage it.

Said one of Lisa Marie's friends: "Right now Lisa Marie is trying to sort out her mind."

Michael Jackson himself had no such problem
with his mind. He had made his mind up, and what
he wanted to do was to have children. He did not
seem bothered that he had left Lisa Marie in bad
mental shape. During their marriage he had upset
her with extensive reports in the media about how he
was cavorting with young boys all the while he was
away from her.

A video even surfaced that showed Michael
romping away on the amusement rides and the
swings and monkey bars at Neverland with three
handsome preadolescent boys. Not only that, but
during his marriage to Lisa Marie another scandal
emerged in the tabloids in which it was claimed that
the mother of another 13-year-old boy said she had
shown Michael Jackson a compromising video of the
superstar acting inappropriately in a sexual manner
with her son. Reports held that Jacko had paid the
woman off for the video and her silence. If true, this
was a wise move on the part of Jackson, since the
cases against him for child molestation were still
open in Los Angeles and in Santa Barbara. The
statute of limitations on these charges would not
expire until the year 2000, so Jackson had to be
careful not to end up in court and, from there, if
convicted, in jail.

That he had involved Lisa Marie in a lawsuit did
not seem to bother Michael either. As a result of
her marriage to Michael, Lisa Marie was named
as a defendant when Evan Chandler sued Diane
Sawyer, ABC, Michael himself and wife Lisa Marie.
Chandler claimed correctly untrue statements had
been promulgated about him and his family as a

result of the infamous Primetime Live interview Diane Sawyer conducted with Michael and Lisa Marie on June 14, 1995. The lawsuit upset Lisa Marie greatly and she was highly relieved when the judge on the case dismissed her own liability. But husband at the time Michael didn't seem to care a whit about involving her in something that potentially embarrassing, if not out-and-out sordid.

But now Michael had new plans and schemes. He had decided to have children. This possibility had been bandied about in the press all the while he was married to Lisa Marie, but the two never had a child.

This, in retrospect, must have been a big relief for Lisa Marie when the marriage fell apart. In any event, Michael now had plans to have a child. He had even picked out the mother-to-be. It was none other than the medical assistant he had known for years in the office of his Beverly Hills dermatologist, Dr. Arnold Klein.

Her name was Debbie Rowe and she was originally Australian. She had previously been married to a computer whiz, but that hadn't worked out, and she had been living alone in an inexpensive apartment in Van Nuys, California, and commuting to work in Beverly Hills. She fancied herself a very special woman to Michael. She had known him for 15 years and she is reported to have boasted to friends that she was the only woman alive to have seen Michael Jackson naked with the exception of his mother Katherine. That is, until Michael allegedly broke her heart by marrying Lisa Marie Presley.

Debbie claimed that when Jackson married Lisa Marie , she was shattered by it, since she was said to have had a major crush on him for years. There were articles out when Debbie and Michael first became a news item that reported that Debbie had built a veritable shrine to Michael in her small apartment. She had posters of him and backstage passes to all of his concerts around the world fastened to her walls. When Michael visited Dr. Klein for treatments, Debbie was supposedly the only person allowed to touch him other than the dermatologist himself.

Debbie and Jacko reportedly fell madly in love even while Michael was still married to Lisa Marie. Debbie stated that Michael was distraught that he and Lisa Marie had not been able to have a child. She said that he called her one night and told her how lonely he was. She volunteered to come and relieve his loneliness and he sent a limo for her. When she arrived at Neverland they were soon in an embrace that was quickly followed by a passionate trip to the bedroom, where they made mad love. Debbie said, as they hugged and kissed, she whispered: "Michael, I could give you a child. Let me try to get pregnant." His response, according to her? "Tears of joy were streaming down his face as we went to his bedroom and started to make love."

Debbie went on to say that Michael was a fantastic lover, once he got started. The thing of it was, that he had to dress up to get turned on. Once he had dressed up in a suit of armor so he could play a knight conquering a peasant girl, the peasant girl played of course by the pliant Debbie. Another time Jacko dressed as a pirate.

Debbie told a friend: "He explained he had to dress up to get turned on. It made him feel romantic." She also said Jacko was quite the cavalier and considerate lover at other times. For instance, he would scatter rose petals on the bed. He would burn candles and incense and fill the room with erotic fragrances. Of course he could go the other way and be raucous and dramatic. Once the lights in the bedroom started flashing and the music from Thriller began blaring from the sound system. Next Michael appeared wearing one of his patented costumes, the ones reputed to turn him on like a latter day Valentino. Few will believe this rigamarole when subsequent events are factored into the equation. Debbie sounds like an intelligent and well-paid shill, and yet another sexual beard, but this one assigned the role of breeder as well.

When she was six months into her pregnancy, Debbie reportedly demanded that Michael marry her and legitimize their child. This Michael duly did while he was on tour in Australia. A judge married the couple in a civil ceremony minutes past midnight in a suite at the Sheraton on the Park Hotel in Sydney on November 15, 1996. Debbie was angry within mere minutes. She told a friend that "Here I was marrying my idol whose baby kicked inside me, and it seemed he wanted to gallop through the ceremony in double-time."

Although Michael gave her a platinum two-and-a-half carat diamond ring, he didn't want a ring from her. And when the judge pronounced them man and wife in the hotel suite, Debbie said: "I turned to Michael expecting a big kiss, but all I got was a little peck on the cheek." She was instantly in for a bigger shock. He also didn't want to sleep with her in the same bed on their wedding night — or even in the same room. That night in the Sheraton Debbie Rowe slept alone in a $3,000-a-night suite, where it was reported that she cried herself to sleep. She told friends back in the States: "My honeymoon night with Michael was the most disappointing night of my life!"

The next night wasn't much better. Michael was spending lots of time with a new special friend, an 8-year-old boy named Anthony. Michael claimed the boy was his nephew, but of course Michael Jackson has no nephew named Anthony. Michael was scheduled that night to attend the opening of the movie "Ghosts." Debbie thought she would be his escort. She thought wrong. He told her to stay put in the hotel. He said the crowds might jostle her and injure their unborn child. No, he would attend the opening of "Ghosts" with his new friend Anthony, his putative nephew. This he did, and was widely photographed with the boy beside him.

The following day, Debbie again hoped for some face time with her new husband, but it was not to be. He had other plans. He took Anthony and visited Sydney's famous Taronga Zoo. Debbie is reported to have told a close friend back in the States: "I think I may have made the biggest mistake of my life — and the only way out of it is divorce."

Bear in mind that this insight on Debbie's part is alleged to have occurred to her a scant 72 hours after her wedding ceremony. If this account of her wedding to Michael Jackson is all true, and it would appear to be, it makes his first bare-bones wedding ceremony with Lisa Marie Presley in the Dominican Republic look like a royal wedding by comparison.

But something is all out of round with this entire Debbie Rowe affair. It was revealed that Debbie had been a biker chick who roared around Los Angeles clad in leather outfits on a Harley-Davidson and wanting to be a Hell's Angel. She was alleged to have shocked even hardcore bikers with her foul language, and she used to love to swill beer and tequila and then intimidate men with her vulgar, in-your-face challenges. Her use of profanity is interesting in that the Gloved One is on record as loathing the use of foul language, yet another legacy of his Jehovah's Witness past.

New wife Debbie apparently had been adopted and raised by wealthy parents who lived in an expensive house in Malibu, though she took no money from them and lived alone in her small and dark apartment in Van Nuys. But even this article reiterated that Debbie had turned her small pad into a shrine to Michael Jackson.

So she was either this devoted groupie type of ditz or she was a clever businesswoman willing to exchange breeding privileges for several million dollars.

As always with Wacko Jacko, it is hard to get at the truth here — so it is best to simply report both sides of the story. Still, the side that seems right is the one that has Debbie making a business deal with Jackson to serve as a surrogate mother, and he was about to become a father.

On February 13, 1997, Debbie Rowe gave birth to Michael Jackson's son, named Prince Michael. The boy was named for Michael's grandfather and great-grandfather. Stories quickly appeared in the press relating how heartbroken Debbie was that father Michael took the baby from her immediately, telling her, "Don't get too attached to him, Debbie."

Michael was set on raising his son by himself and mostly in France, if reports were to be believed. There were soon screaming headlines that Michael had stolen the baby from Debbie. But these stories were countered by reports that Debbie had a marriage contract with Michael that was closer to an employment contract than anything to do with a conjugal arrangement as it's usually structured. According to these reports, Debbie received a million dollars for having Michael's son. She was to receive an additional million dollars if she had a second child. There were also escalators in the deal that would pay Debbie more money the longer she stayed married to Michael.

Yet there were accounts of how distressed Debbie became over the treatment Michael accorded her. He took the baby boy from her immediately after its birth and traveled with the baby to the Neverland Ranch. At the same time, he insisted that Debbie stay away. In fact, he demanded that she leave the L.A. area. She protested and ended up going on vacation to Arizona. But she refused to follow Michael's instructions to dye her hair and cut it short in order to move about incognito. In the weeks following the baby's birth, Debbie was deliberately frozen out from any communication with him. Michael simply gave her reports over the phone that the baby was healthy and doing well. Eventually, Debbie went back to her job working as a medical assistant for Dr. Arnold Klein, Michael's Beverly Hills dermatologist.

There were repeated rumors that Michael treated Debbie as an employee and never as a wife. He avoided her in public. He went out by himself. He instructed his staff not to refer to her as "Mrs. Jackson" but only as "Miss Rowe." When Prince Michael Jr. was 2 months old, Michael Jackson summoned Debbie to join him at a Beverly Hills hotel for a photoshoot. This session turned into a six-page exclusive spread in the National Enquirer published April 28, 1997. But Michael Jackson didn't treat Debbie Rowe any better after the photo session than he had before it. Again, according to sources, he quickly banished her, virtually excluding her from contact with her son.

Michael had for years referred to women with contempt according to those close to him. One of his favorite words of contempt for women was to call them "heifers." He was clearly treating Debbie as a heifer.

As stated earlier, Debbie is either a clever businesswoman or a foolish groupie of some kind. But the probability is that she is the former. Stories appeared during the time of her marriage that she was still dating old boyfriends and going out frequently herself. Michael apparently liked and encouraged this, according to some reports. According to other sources, this type of behavior on Debbie's part was strictly forbidden by the "marriage" contract between Michael and her. For Michael's part, you can guess what happened.

There were more and more stories about new special young male friends. Less than a year after the birth of Michael's son, there were reports that Jackson, now legally a father, was appearing in public with another young boy named Omar Bhatti. Michael was described as lavishing gifts on the boy and on his family in general.

It was the old pattern again. Shower the kid with gifts. Bury his family in luxury compared to what they had been used to. Dress the kid in designer outfits, with lots of them matching Micheal's outfits. Make sure many of the clothes the kid wore made him look like a smaller version of a toy soldier than Michael's larger version. Michael had met Omar while on tour in Tunisia. Three years earlier, Omar had made quite a hit in Scandinavia by doing his very polished imitation of the Gloved One.

Whatever was going on here, with Michael's marriage to Debbie Rowe, it was magno-bizarro, completely in keeping with the Wacko Jacko life story. Because only 14 months after Debbie gave birth to Prince Michael, she bore Michael Jackson's daughter Paris-Michael Katherine Jackson on April 3, 1998. The new baby was born at the Spalding Pain Medical Clinic in Beverly Hills, and not, as their son had been, at Cedars-Sinai.

There were reports by this time circulating

widely that Michael Jackson was hurting for money. Maybe the way daughter Paris came into the world lends some credence to these reports. Prince Michael Jr. had been born on the VIP floor at Cedars-Sinai. His father Michael Jackson had rented the entire floor for the occasion. But now that daughter Paris came along, father Michael Jackson had only arranged a room in a modest clinic. And, whereas there had been a whole host of security guards present when the boy was born 14 months earlier, when his little sister was born there was only one guard present.

But Michael Jackson repeated his earlier pattern and took the baby girl immediately from its mother. He again became the sole caregiver for the child, though he reportedly had hired a raft of nurses and nannies to help him out. He also imported his mother Katherine to the Neverland Ranch to help raise his children.

But, make no mistake, it appears as if their birth mother was banished. There was a crazy incident in 1999 where son Prince Michael had a routine seizure that was competently handled by the boy's doctor, yet his father had it put out on the news wires that the boy had nearly died. Mother Debbie in Los Angeles learned all of this from televised news reports and became hysterical. It soon appeared that Jackson had exaggerated his son's illness in order to avoid traveling to Modena, Italy, to perform on stage at a concert to benefit charity with tenor Luciano Pavarotti. Pavarotti, compassionately, had the audience at the concert pray for Michael Jackson's supposedly dying son.

It was also reported that Michael Jackson himself was back on painkillers. Jackson was regularly connected to an intravenous drip that fed him large doses of the powerful painkiller Demerol. There was speculation that Jackson might once again be addicted to such painkillers.

To add to the general air of craziness that always seems to surround him, more stories emerged in the press about videos surfacing that showed the singer playing in the private garden at Neverland with two and three adolescent boys at a time, often with their shirts off. Michael would clown with them on the merry-go-round or on the jungle gym. He often liked to videotape these youngsters at play. This private video collection of Michael's had apparently driven his ex-wife Lisa Marie to real anger when she discovered it.

There were now two children Michael Jackson called his own, but the old patterns of cuckoo behavior on the part of Wacko Jacko went right on as they had before.

Nothing seemed to really be changed, or probably ever would be.

———

Michael Jackson did a good job of hiding his two children from the media glare. He did not want them publicized at all. Then, in September of 2000, a photograph the two children as they played in a limousine outside a hotel where they had stayed the night before. Neither of the children seems to bear any resemblance to their putative father. In fact, Prince Michael Jr. has very light blond hair.

There had been earlier whispers that the Jackson family did not relate to Michael's children. What's more, there had been rumors that the children were not really Michael's and that they were the products of artificial insemination.

As early as December 1996, Debbie's dad Gordon Rowe expressed outrage that anyone would believe that his daughter was pregnant by Michael Jackson the natural way. In the reports, Gordon Rowe said that his daughter called and informed him that she was going to have Michael Jackson's baby. When her father recovered from the shock of this news, she told him on the phone: "Come on, it's not so bad. We had the child by artificial insemination."

Her dad was displeased by this, and said: "Debbie, why artificial insemination? Isn't he capable of fathering a child like anyone else?"

She laughed and replied: "Michael doesn't do anything like anyone else."

These artificial insemination theories seemed to be substantiated three years later when it was leaked that Debbie Rowe had told friends that: "I am just the vehicle carrying the baby."

It was claimed that Debbie's marriage was scheduled to last six years, but that she couldn't take it any longer. Her contract with Michael Jackson, according to sources, verified the reports that it had strictures in it that would not permit her to be seen in public with other men, and she could no longer hack this abstemious lifestyle. She moved out of her small apartment and into a nice house costing more than a million dollars on the periphery of Beverly Hills, which she purchased with money from Michael, according to reliable sources.

Then Rowe filed for divorce from Jackson in October of 1999. According to insiders, she received a divorce settlement from Michael that paid her $36 million over six years. Of course, the payoff came replete with a gag order. If Debbie discussed any aspect of her relationship with Michael Jackson or her marriage and child bearing activities under his direction, she would forfeit the settlement.

So there is clearly evidence that suggests that Prince Michael Jackson Jr. and his sister Paris-Michael Katherine Jackson are the products of biological engineering. No one can really say for sure what is true in this regard and what is not, but the evidence is quite convincing that artificial insemination took place and that the Gloved One did not biologically father the children.

All anyone can be sure of with Michael Jackson is that anything is possible — he wouldn't hesitate a nanosecond to create a family along the lines of Brave New World.

It wouldn't be surprising to learn that Michael Jackson had tried to clone himself in male and female versions, both, complements of futuristic biological engineering, rendered white. The two children could even be a kind of Victor/Victoria experiment in artificial breeding for all anyone knows.

The word "bizarre" in the dictionary should have a picture of Wacko Jacko beside it.

One thing is certain — suffer the children may be

the only relevant sentiment where the fates and futures of Prince Michael Jr. and Paris-Michael are concerned.

"The message this sends is disgusting: 'If you're rich, you can abuse children.' Also, I think that if you're innocent, you don't give someone millions." — Raoul Felder, famous NYC attorney on the Chandler affair settlement in February 1994.

CHAPTER 13

Today Michael Jackson is a ruined man. He and his people have made many attempts to mend his image but they have all failed. He is no longer perceived as sweet and shy, sensitive and talented. He is no longer seen as the little boy who charmed the world but as the man-child who interferes with little boys, to use a Victorian word for sexual molestation.

He is an object of ridicule in the popular press. People who once mobbed him now shun him. He goes through life wearing disguises and dressing as an Arab woman and it is all tearfully pathetic. In public he shrouds his two children in blankets and shields them from reality, just as he, as a child, was shielded from reality by the brutal exploitation of his individuality and talents by his family, especially his father, in the interests of earning money.

Over the years there have even been savage evaluations of his music and his legacy. In 1987, he was roundly dismissed and disrespected by the readers of Rolling Stone magazine. They voted him that year as the winner (read loser) in not fewer than eight categories of failure. Among the embarrassing categories he won, he polled the most votes for worst male singer, worst dressed, worst single for "Bad," worst album for Bad, worst video for Bad, and for having the worst hype and being the entertainer whose comeback would receive the chilliest reception.

Against this you have to balance the assessment of no less an authority than the great Quincy Jones, who, in his autobiography *Q*, had this to say about Michael Jackson: "Most child stars never make it beyond kid stardom, but Michael was different. I'll always love him. Today the writers and critics seem determined to try to write him out of history, but it ain't gonna happen. That's why they call it history. Elvis got strange; so did others, later in their careers. Michael Jackson has his place in pop history — at the top, no matter what anybody says about the Eagles surpassing him in domestic sales or how eccentric he's become. When it comes to worldwide sales, Michael is the man to beat."

Musically, the truth surely lies somewhere between these two extremes, but on a personal basis, the decision is much clearer. Many people think Michael Jackson is a very sick person and desperately in need of psychiatric help to overcome his sexual addiction to young boys.

The weekend these words are being written started off Friday, November 15, 2002, with these headlines. The New York Daily News trumpeted, "Wacko Jacko's Nutty Nose Job" and followed with a prominent story on page five. At the same time, the New York Post blared, "Jacko's Nose Out of Joint" and ran a featured story on page three.

Both papers ran cover photos of Michael Jackson, and both reported that a photo of him taken the previous Wednesday in a Santa Barbara court showed that his nose was disintegrating. The photo, when posted on the Internet, was reported to have drawn millions of viewers. According to the accompanying Post story, written by David K. Li, Michael Jackson found himself in court because German concert promoter Marcel Avram was suing him. The promoter claimed Jackson reneged on an agreement to perform two millennium concerts on New Year's Eve of 1999. Jackson countered that the promoter had canceled the concerts in a phone call to him. Not so, according to Avram: He maintained that Michael Jackson was a no-show because of prior recording commitments.

Jackson argued that performing both concerts was not possible anyway because they were timed too closely together. "That would have been tough," Michael said. "Every show I lose fifteen pounds."

He further stated that he was weighed before and after each show, and that his performances had to be spaced out for health reasons. About his involvement with business affairs concerning MJJ Productions, Michael, after stating that he got only an overview of business matters from his advisers, was quoted this way in the Post: "I'm in the creative department. I'm a visionary."

In the story in the News, written by Alev Aktar, the paper's fashion and beauty editor, there was much serious discussion of the damage Michael had done to his face through excessive and abusive overuse of plastic surgery. The paper ran a series of six photos taken previous to the photograph snapped in the Santa Barbara court on Wednesday, November 13, 2002. They showed the progression in Michael's looks from 1972 through 1998 as he altered himself through plastic surgery. He went, of course, from being a really handsome African-American kid to looking like some kind of goony freak.

Above this series of smaller progressive photos the News juxtaposed a quarter-page blowup of the infamous shot taken two days earlier in California. This blowup photo was indexed and showed the extent of Michael's facial plastic surgery under the subheadline: "Experts Say There's Nothing He Hasn't Had Done." The indexed boxes illustrated the extent of the plastic surgeries, including: Botox injections to the forehead; tattooed eyebrows; reconstructive work done to his nose after numerous rhinoplasties damaged its tissue; chemical bleaching to his skin; extensive eye work, possibly including tattooed eyeliner; hair straightening or the use of a wig, and scalp replacement surgery. This final surgery would have been a legacy of the burns incurred in the Pepsi commercial explosion and fire in 1984.

In the article, Michael's former plastic surgeon, Dr. Steven Hoefflin of Santa Monica, denied

responsibility for the way Jacko looked. A lawyer for
Dr. Hoefflin, Karen Cotler, was quoted in the article:
"Dr. Steven Hoefflin has not done any of Michael
Jackson's nasal surgery since 1998, and had advised
him against further surgery."

The News article also quoted Dr. Gerald Imber, a
prominent Manhattan plastic surgeon: "Clearly, he
had some sort of nasal-tip disaster. What probably
happened is that he had some sort of support put in
there and the tissue broke down. Now, it looks like
he has skin grafts or something to close it up. A
collapsed nose is very unusual — I've never seen one,
and I've done fifteen thousand rhinoplasties."

A dermatologist quoted in this same article,
Dr. Dennis Gross, said that it looked like Michael
Jackson had undertaken a permanent skin lightening
treatment using some chemical mixture based on
hydroquinone, a chemical whose use, he said, was
banned in the U.S.

Yet another New York City dermatologist quoted
in the article, Dr. Pat Wexler, stated that doctors
had a responsibility to refuse a patient treatment
when that patient was obviously being excessive.
Dr. Wexler, quite laudably, said that the operative
word was a simple "No," and doctors had to
sometimes use it. But it is doubtful that a
strong-willed man like Michael Jackson will accept
that kind of negative response from anyone as long as
he has the money to force his will to be done. As a
result, he has rendered himself, in terms of plastic
surgery and dermatology, a total freak.

The press has pointed this out, and likewise has
underscored the weird way he has gone about raising

his two children, who never see their mother, Debbie. They are isolated from other children their age. They are never allowed out to play. All of their toys are used once and then donated to charity for fear the toys will become contaminated with germs. This holds true for other things as well, such as household items like utensils, spoons, glasses and bottles. Each child has two nannies and a nurse is supposed to always be available.

The kids get everything they want — except a normal life.

When they are taken outside, Michael usually wraps them in blankets or sheets to foil the efforts of photographers to snap pictures of them. It is said that the children will not attend schools when they are old enough to do so. Instead, they will be tutored at home. Again, this is to avoid the possibilities that they will come into contact with germs. Said a source in a position to know about Michael Jackson: "His whole life now revolves around his two children and he doesn't want any other adult, certainly not Debbie, telling him how to bring them up." Contemplate how sad that is, and how potentially tragic for the children.

So it is fairly clear that these two children will be traumatized in their development. They have no mother in their lives. They interact with no children their own ages. They don't go outside unless chaperoned. They move around outdoors with sheets and blankets over their heads.

It is interesting, given the history of Michael's abusive upbringing and the history of dysfunction in the Jackson family, that he has eliminated a mother from his children's lives. It is interesting as well from this perspective that he has, obviously in his own mind, cast himself as the perfect father, biological realities aside. It is interesting that, if reports are true, he human-engineered a sister for son Prince Michael but no brothers, given the troubled history he had with his own brothers.

What is sad beyond telling is that Michael Jackson, perhaps as well-meaning as his own parents were in raising him, is doing things for his two children that in all likelihood they will resent him for and, when their turn comes, characterize as child abuse.

So once again you see the cyclical nature of child abuse in action.

———

At this point in Michael Jackson's life, it is clear, to everyone but him that he has destroyed his credibility and wrecked his image. He has certainly been clever and assiduous in trying to change that image. Yet the two marriages are a joke. One looked like an elaborate publicity stunt and the other looked like an even more elaborate publicity stunt combined with a contract to breed. Neither appears to have changed the perception of Michael Jackson as a pedophile.

Nor had the perception of him changed even as far back as when he was bearding himself with Tatum O'Neal and Brooke Shields. He may have kissed Lisa Marie Presley on the lips at the MTV Awards, just as he kissed Brooke Shields years ago in a limousine for photographers from around the world to record, but none of this mattered. Madonna came out and said that he did not respond to her sexual advances. This was exactly what was said earlier by the sexy model and dancer Tatiana Thumbtzen, who claimed that she tried everything to get Michael to respond to her sexually, but he never did.

As Tatiana said: "The writing was on the wall. I knew that when Michael started hanging around with a boy. He liked the kid so much I heard he gave his family a million dollars, fancy clothes, exotic vacations and a Rolls-Royce. He made it clear he preferred the kid's company to mine. But when I read he'd paid out so many millions to the little boy in the sex-abuse case — while still protesting his innocence — it somehow had a hollow ring. It's as if he wanted people to think he was an all-American, red-blooded male, that one day he'd find a mate, get married, have kids, that I would have had his babies. But deep down in his heart he knows he never will."

Look what happened to his credibility when he addressed the world for four minutes on CNN on December 22, 1993, protesting his innocence. We saw previously that world famous lie-detector expert Charles R. McQuiston said that Michael Jackson was not telling the truth. So, too, did Stephen Laub, who runs the Truth Verification Laboratory outside of New York City. He had analyzed voice stress tests for prosecutors and police departments for decades. He stated: "My opinion is that he's not innocent of the allegations that there were some improprieties with children." After speculating that the speech Michael gave that night was scripted, Laub added:

"He himself doesn't believe what he was saying."

Indeed, most of the people in this world agreed with these experts on lying. They did not believe Michael Jackson's version of reality either. The same public reaction resulted from the Diane Sawyer interview on Primetime Live on June 14, 1995. Nobody really believed Michael Jackson was coming clean with the truth and nothing but the truth.

The same response occurred when Jackson bonded with O.J. Simpson as an innocent man victimized by racism. There were reports that Jacko lent more than a million dollars to O.J., and that he wrote a sympathetic letter to Simpson in prison during the former football great's media-circus trial. Jackson made statements to the effect that he settled with the Chandlers to avoid the kind of trial that O.J. Simpson had to endure. It was even reported that Simpson had brought his children Sydney and Justin to Neverland a few times so that they could visit the amusement park and watch movies with Michael in the video room. To the press, Michael gave statements portraying both Simpson and himself as black men whose success riled white people to the point where both black celebrities had to be yanked down and dragged through the mud for reasons based on racial jealousy and bias. This didn't wash with the general public either. Nobody took it seriously.

The same thing happened in July of 2002, when Michael attacked Sony for the failure of his latest album, Invincible. Michael joined a crosstown march led by the Reverend Al Sharpton in Manhattan to protest the racism in the music industry. He even went so far as to ride around Midtown on the open upper deck of a double decker bus holding a placard depicting Sony boss Tommy Mottola as the devil. In the press, Michael blasted Mottola as "devilish" and "racist."

These characterizations of Tommy Mottola took everyone in the music industry by surprise. They felt that Michael was reacting to the failure of his latest album and not to anything Sony or Mottola had failed to do for him or for that album. On the contrary, Sony and Mottola had backed the Invincible album to the tune of $60 million. But it flopped, that's the whole story. It sold just two million copies or, to put it in perspective, a mere five percent of what Thriller had sold two decades earlier.

A music insider was quoted regarding Michael's protest against Sony and Tommy Mottola to this effect: "Michael finally flipped and it's cost him what few friends he had left among music's power people. What he did was commit career suicide, plain and simple." This insider later added: "What Michael did was try to make it seem as if he was dumping Tommy rather than the other way around. The failure of Invincible made Michael realize he was all washed up and he desperately wanted to save face."

Michael no doubt wanted to save face as well with all of the articles appearing in the press claiming that he was nearly broke. There were rumors that people were suing him for bills that had gone unpaid, even for his hospital bill for the delivery of his son Prince Michael Jr. A Beverly Hills jeweler had sued Michael over an 18th-century watch he agreed to buy for just under a million and a half dollars. But Michael used the watch for six months and then returned it, never having paid for it. It was scratched and obviously used, so the luxury jeweler sued. Another news item reported that two former Michael Jackson financial advisers were suing him for non-payment of their monthly fees. Stories in the press speculated that Michael needed $14 million a year just to run the Neverland Valley Ranch. His monthly personal expenses were also estimated at $8 million. In light of such revelations, it was easy to see how he could be going broke.

In the end, all of Michael Jackson's spin moves didn't work. It was as bad as the move the entire Jackson family had made back in early 1994, when they sought to rehabilitate Michael's image after the Jordie Chandler scandal had just been settled out of court. They broadcast on television a show called the Jackson Family Honors and the whole thing devolved into a farce. Michael had threatened that night not even to go on the show, but of course his mother Katherine laid down the law and he duly went on stage with his brothers and sisters. But the show was panned. What was even worse, reports later circulated that the Jacksons had misappropriated funds connected with the show that were earmarked for charitable causes. This whole public relations production, the Jackson Family Honors, backfired, and the Jacksons and Michael were panned in the press.

Everything connected these days to Michael Jackson seems cheap or ridiculous or in some way tawdry. Everything presently coming out about him

is as laughable as the report that made the rounds
after Michael had been in rehab in late 1993
and early 1994. That's when his detractors said he
was merely hiding out in rehab abroad to avoid
prosecution back home in California on the child
molestation charges brought against him by the
Chandlers.

According to insiders, some counselors at the
Charter Nightingale Clinic in London claimed back
then that patient Michael Jackson was a virgin and
therefore could not possibly have had sexual relations
with young Jordan Chandler or with anyone else.
This is patently absurd on their part and shows a
woeful lack of knowledge of human nature, human
psychology and even human anatomy. Maybe these
counselors must have been as confused about what
constituted sexual activity as former President
William Jefferson Clinton had been.

An insider at the Nightengale Clinic was quoted as
saying about this team who evaluated Michael
Jackson in rehab: "There is absolutely no doubt in
the team's mind that Jackson is totally innocent.
His sexy stage act and raunchy videos are just a
performance and have no sexual effect whatsoever on
him." If the public agreed with this assessment of
Jacko from the Sceptered Isle, they also believed that
pigs can fly and goats ought to shave.

And what continued through all of this? Yes,
reports that Michael Jackson was keeping close
company with a succession of young male special
friends. There were many, many stories to this effect
in the press. Michael, as usual, was flaunting his
preference for the companionship of young boys

and, like the addict he is, he was defiant about it.

Then in August 2002, it was reported that Michael's family had attempted an intervention with him. They feared from reports given to them by members of Michael's staff that he was seriously back on painkillers and booze, apparently mixing Demerol with wallops of wine. Some alleged that this regime of vino and painkillers explained his recent outlandish behavior toward Sony and Tommy Mottola. Members of Michael's family feared that he would turn up dead just the way Elvis Presley had.

This is, of course, how Michael Jackson came to be the sad and tearful figure slumped into a sofa trying to interest visiting New York City publishers in a book that would set the record straight and rehabilitate his image. This was the Michael Jackson so lacking in self-awareness that he really thought book publishers would be interested in a children's book from him. This was Michael Jackson on August 28, 2002, at the Westin Hotel in Stamford, Connecticut.

Jackson was a man who only weeks before had made a public display of himself in protesting Sony and Tommy Mottola's lack of professionalism because his latest album, Invincible, had tanked terribly. He was a man who was only a few days away from being embarrassed on national television at the MTV Awards when Britney Spears, in an offhand remark, referred to him as the "entertainer of the millennium." When he reacted to her words as though they conferred an official award when they were, in fact, merely a tossed off remark and a hyped up compliment, he was ridiculed and mocked in the press.

It seems these days, he's mostly an object of curiosity or contempt.

Like Peter Pan looking for his shadow, Michael Jackson, like all abused children, was looking for something to make him feel whole and fulfilled. But he couldn't find it. And he would never find it short of undertaking an intense regimen of psychotherapy.

What he did find in his futile search for that magic something that would make him happy was that it's very easy to go from the very top to the very bottom in one swift move. One quick tumble and he went from being the King of Pop to the Sultan of Flop.

Michael Jackson in the new millennium was nothing but a gargantuan freak.

———

When you see Michael Jackson perform on the Dangerous tour, before the Chandler scandal broke, it is a total thrill. He is a showman gifted beyond the powers of anyone to describe. He has to be seen in his prime to be fully appreciated as the genius entertainer he is. Viewing on television the video of the Dangerous tour performance in Bucharest, Romania, right before Michael Jackson's world fell apart, is exhilarating. He dazzled the audience, many of whom fainted from heat prostration, delirium, overexcitement, and just plain emotionalism run amok. They were carried out of the stadium on stretchers and taken to a first aid station. Thousands in the audience sang along with him with tears rolling down their cheeks. Many of their faces held a stunned look, an otherworldly look. On stage, Michael Jackson danced and gyrated and sang with abandon. He had the entire stadium of people in a tizzy of ecstasy. He himself was on top of the world.

A Michael Jackson concert like the one in Bucharest for Dangerous had a pronounced religious component to it, almost like a revival meeting. Even the lyrics of some of the songs contained references to theology, to love, to divinity. Michael Jackson seemed to work an audience as well as Elmer Gantry or any preacher, politician or demagogue who ever lived. During the Bucharest concert, when he sang "Heal the World," a giant globe descended onto the stage and rested beside him. You had to tune in to Michael's religious bent when he voiced such lyrics from "Heal the World" as: "And the dream we were conceived in will reveal a joyful face/And the world we once believed in will shine again in grace."

The song's lyrics also exhort everyone to "Be God's Glow." Michael Jackson's early childhood devotion to the Jehovah's Witness faith is never far from his consciousness. It's conceivable during his wretched childhood, when he was exploited and tortured by his too early and too heavy employment in the entertainment business, that Kingdom Hall represented the only spiritual sunbeam in a life that was too early on nothing but a dreary commercial slog. With the Jehovah's Witnesses, young Michael Jackson wasn't exploited for his talent but valued merely for himself. That experience marked him for life and shines forth in all of his artistry. Even when he's acting onstage like a repulsive sex-obsessed fool, he is never far from his religious training, no matter that he's sometimes rejecting its too tight sexual strictures and inhibitions. Religion owns his soul.

In 1988, Michael is quoted as saying about God: "He actually appears before me in a vision. I can talk to Him and even reach out and touch His robe. When I'm onstage I can see a tall figure materialize before me, smiling at me and encouraging me to keep going." He added, "Without God appearing to me, I couldn't handle the incredible strain of a two-hour show."

A friend of Michael's is quoted about Michael's relationship to God: "He believes that God put him on earth for a special purpose. Talking to God seems quite normal to him." That is, as mentioned previously, Michael Jackson sees himself, delusional or not, as a messiah. He thinks he is on earth to proselytize for the triumph of divine love over all strife and hardship and adversity. It's an admirable fantasy.

That's why it's not surprising, near the end of the Dangerous performance in Bucharest, to see a large angel descend from above the stage and enfold Michael Jackson in its oversized wings. This is more or less symbolic of his lifelong quest to find true mothering, nurturing mothering, mothering that wasn't harsh, possessive, domineering and over-controlling. Much of the impulse symbolized on stage by the giant angel is behind Michael's quest in his early years to turn himself into Diana Ross and, in more recent years, to be consumed and smothered with maternal love by Elizabeth Taylor. He is nothing if not a little boy lost. A little boy in search of a true childhood to replace the blighted and profaned and exploited one he actually had to live through.

But Michael Jackson has always been in denial and has always missed the point.

In a 52-page booklet that accompanied the album of HIStory, he included a line drawing of a self-portrait. It showed him as a young boy cowering in a corner holding a microphone. He has both hands tucked under his tightly crossed arms. It's as though he anticipates that he might reach out and do things with his hands that he shouldn't, that might be sinful, that would violate the teachings of the Jehovah's Witnesses.

What's more, the whole portrait is an attempt to negate an adulthood, and actions he's taken as an adult, that he can't handle. It is, yet again, a plea for understanding of his life and his ruinous childhood. It is a plea for compassion and a plea for help, on one hand. On the other hand, it is casting Michael Jackson as an innocent and misunderstood victim. This is revolting because he is anything but that. It is really dreary and sad, especially when you consider the spectacular ending to the Dangerous performance in Bucharest.

At the end of the concert, Michael Jackson dons a spaceman's uniform and blasts off, actually leaving the stadium as though he were propelled upward by the jets attached to the back of his spaceman's outfit. Like his hero Peter Pan, he flies away, something he has always talked of doing since his early childhood days. And he presumably flies off to explore outer space, something of another lifelong dream of his. But Jackson's problem is that he has explored, or wanted to explore, in the wrong direction. He needed to put some of the fortune he squandered on plastic surgery into improving the inside of his head. He needed to explore inner space.

This fantasy quest of his for the perfect self-image underscores the fundamental mistake Michael Jackson has made in life. We now turn to a top research psychiatrist named Dr. David Veale, who is an expert on a form of mental illness known as Body Dismorphic Disorder, or BDD.

BDD is a condition in which its sufferers see only their faults and flaws when they look in the mirror. They are known to spend hours in front of a mirror obsessing over what they perceive to be an imperfection in their looks. All teenagers seem to go through a stage something like this, but usually in a mild form. In BDD victims, the condition is acute. They are dissatisfied with their looks and obsessed with getting them right, with fixing them. It is a mental condition that can afflict even people as good-looking as Michael Jackson was before he ever visited a plastic surgeon or a dermatologist. It is a sick form of mental obsession — like a hideous case of "Don't Stop 'Til You Get Enough" applied wrong and taken to a hurtful extreme. In the article, Dr. Veale suggested that Michael Jackson could probably find relief for his mentally anguished condition in two forms of treatment. One would be in the use of antidepressant drugs and the other would be in therapy sessions with a competent psychiatrist or psychologist.

There is no doubt that Dr. Veale is right. There is ample evidence that Jackson himself spoke about this problem openly in group sessions while he was a patient at the Charter Nightingale Clinic in

London detoxing from the abuse of painkillers and tranquilizers. It's clear that no one told Michael when he was a child that he was wonderful and handsome and quite fine the way he looked. On the contrary, he was maltreated and abused and the results are not pretty. He has always, most certainly, been suffering from untreated clinical depression. He has tortured himself unnecessarily over what he believes are his inadequate or second-rate looks.

In the past Jackson has wrapped himself up as a mummy, covering himself from head to toe in winding cloth, like a corpse. He has worn surgical masks for years, obscuring most of his face. He has even resorted to wearing clothes that belonged to his idol Diana Ross, including underwear, and dressed frequently as an Arab woman, obscuring all of his bodily parts except his eyes, for which he left slits open so he could see. Michael Jackson, wildly dissatisfied with himself, has resorted to cross-dressing as an extreme remedy for looks he wants to reject.

───────

At the end of each session with the visiting publishers that hot August day in 2002, Michael Jackson would hand out a DVD of his Madison Square Garden Retrospective as a takeaway gift. But today, Michael is shunned by his once adoring public. He who was loved and worshipped by millions is now reviled by millions.

In each of the interviews in Stamford with the visiting New York publishers, to illustrate the horrors of all-encompassing fame such as his, Michael Jackson would state that he was thoroughly bored with himself, with being Michael Jackson.

Apparently he was not alone in this emotion.

Not one of the half dozen or so New York City publishers who visited with him offered to buy his new book proposal. For the first time in his life, Michael Jackson, recipient of the Grammy Living Legend Award in 1993, the very year his downfall began, found himself in a buyer's market.

And ultimately, there were no takers.

A singer and entertainer of Michael Jackson's stature has his discography readily available from many sources, but what is lacking is a catalog of his weirdness, or simply, a "Wackography."

1) Trying to Buy the Elephant Man: Michael bought clothing and artifacts that had belonged to John Merrick, the Victorian man deformed by neurofibromatosis who was called The Elephant Man. Jackson is reported to have even tried to buy John Merrick's bones from the British Museum. Jackson reportedly identified with John Merrick and his freakish condition and the commercial exploitation it led to.

2) Fascination with Freaks: Michael became enthralled with other sideshow freaks of nature. He could discourse for hours on the lives of Siamese twins and bearded ladies and other oddities of standard sideshows, like two-headed babies and such other mistakes of Mother Nature.

3) The Human Brain: Michael's infatuation with anatomy led him to keep a human brain in a jar of formaldehyde in his bedroom. He later added a second brain to his collection. In addition, Michael later traveled to the UCLA Medical Center operating theatre. With a smile on his face, he observed several blood-soaked brain operations, never flinching or becoming queasy.

4) Saving His Own Nose in a Jar: Michael's fixation on keepsakes and anatomy combined to have him store a piece of his nose cartilage in a jar in his room after it was removed in one of his early plastic surgeries.

5) The Pope's Appendix: When the pope had his appendix removed, Michael made a serious offer of $50,000 to buy it.

6) Secret Hideaways: Michael loved to have secret places and passageways, the kind that are popular in classic children's literature. At his family's compound in Encino, Hayvenhurst, Michael had a secret passage built that led outside to the garden. The walls of this secret passageway were lined with children's books. At Neverland Ranch, he notoriously kept the secret playroom to entertain his young male friends. It was tiny and kept in near darkness except for the glow from a television set and had for furniture only an oversize sofa.

7) Talking to Mannequins: In Michael's bedroom at Hayvenhurst, he kept a handful of mannequins that he used to dress in designer outfits. He would converse with the mannequins at length while he dressed them and fussed with their appearance. Besides the mannequin corps in his bedroom, Michael kept an extensive collection of dolls, which he liked to dress up in various ensembles.

8) Michael and E.T.: Above Michael's headboard of his bed at Neverland, Michael has an oil painting depicting him in the center surrounded by five figures he considers his "equals." They are: the Mona Lisa, George Washington, Albert Einstein, E.T. and Abraham Lincoln. In the painting, Michael stands in a Napoleon pose in military drag and sports his signature sequined white glove and aviator shades — as do the other five figures, including E.T.

9) Warding Off Ghosts: Outside Michael's bedroom at Neverland, he has posted mannequins on either side of the doorway dressed up as Sikh Indian guards. Their job is to ward off ghosts and evil spirits. Michael is on the record as saying that he doesn't mind ghosts as long as they stay outside, but he is absolutely opposed to giving them the run of the house.

10) Always Hiding: When Eddie Murphy invited Michael to be in his music video, What's Up With You?, the Gloved One demanded that a tent-like tunnel be built between his trailer and the set to ensure his privacy from people eyeballing him. When Michael visited his dermatologist, Dr. Arnold Klein, people in the office were instructed to put their heads down on their desks and not to dare look at him as he passed through. Once, on a movie set, Michael made the same demands: No one was to look at him directly. When he passed, they were to keep their eyes down at all times.

11) A Circus Bible: Michael once gave both his manager and his lawyer a biography of P.T. Barnum, the legendary impresario and huckster. He told them: "This is going to be my bible. I want my career to be the greatest show on earth." So when he needed a high-profile gimmick to promote Captain Eo, he concocted the stunt of sleeping in a hyperbaric chamber, the kind usually used to heal burn victims. He said this would help him live to be a 150 years old, a goal of his. A photo of him stretched out in the glass-enclosed chamber then ran worldwide.

12) Buying a Mummy: Michael reportedly paid two million pounds sterling (slightly more than $3 million) for a mummified lion cub, along with the mummy of a young Egyptian boy, plus the boy's mummified pets, a lizard and a rat. These relics dated from approximately 400 years before the birth of Jesus Christ. The pets were buried with the boy for luck in the afterlife and so that he wouldn't be lonely.

13) Bubbles the Best Friend: Michael had a pet chimpanzee called Bubbles. There have been many successors since, all named the same. The original Bubbles was stuffed and mounted by Michael. It is a custom with Michael to dress his pet chimps in designer outfits modeled on the ones he wears. He liked to dine alone with Bubbles and to romp with him in the playroom at Hayvenhurst, where Michael sometimes served him high tea, like something out of Alice in Wonderland.

14) Foreseeing His Own Death: Michael supposedly became convinced that he would die in 1998, when he was only just reaching the age of 40. For a while he signed his name and put "1998" after it every time. A rumor spread that Michael believed that the world was going to end in 1998, but this rumor was unsubstantiated.

15) Paranoid Surveillance: Michael felt so nervous about intruders that he had full surveillance equipment installed at Neverland, including such things as small cameras hidden in birdhouses on the grounds. He also had snooping equipment planted throughout the house, some designed to give him early warning of anyone approaching the secret playroom. He was also allegedly able to satisfy his appetite as a gossip and a snoop by having an eavesdropping system installed on the phones.

16) Always Happy: People employed by Michael can lose their jobs by not acting happy enough or smiling all the time.

17) Like a Virgin: The music that blares from the more than 100 loudspeakers placed around the property at Neverland play mostly show tunes and theme music from Disney pictures. Michael's carousel in the amusement park revolves to the tune of Madonna's "Like a Virgin."

18) Kiddie Games: Michael loves to have both water and pillow fights at Neverland with his little friends. He went so far as to build a small fort at Neverland especially for special friend Macaulay Culkin. Michael is also known to be fond of having food fights. He and Elizabeth Taylor once had a food fight on a video set and did $3,000 worth of damage to a trailer.

19) Avoidance of Germs: Michael is so frightened of coming into contact with germs that he often wears a surgical mask. He also wears a glove to protect his hand from contamination with germs. His children's toys, utensils, bottles, and other household items are tossed away after one-time use for the same reason.

20) Interest in the Occult: Michael is deeply interested in magic, in mime, in the occult, and in the black arts. Reports surfaced at one point that Michael wanted to use the occult powers of a medium to channel his father-in-law Elvis Presley in order to get his permission for Michael to marry the King's only daughter and sole heir, Lisa Marie Presley.

21) Staring at Liz Taylor While Naked: Wacko Jacko, as the British press christened him years ago, is morbidly afraid to be seen naked by a woman. When he was strip-searched under the supervision of two Los Angeles Police Department detectives in 1993, he insisted that no woman be present. The police doctor and the official photographer and video camera operator were all men. Throughout the procedure, while he was nude, Michael silently cried while staring at a photograph of best pal Liz Taylor propped on an easel nearby.

22) A Shrine to Liz: Jackson has a shrine to Elizabeth Taylor in his Neverland estate that includes wallpaper that he designed himself (with little Elizabeth Taylor heads all over it) and a screen showing Taylor's movies 24 hours a day.

23) Wanting to be Diana Ross: Michael's obsession

with Diana Ross is well-documented. He wanted to look just like her, and his initial massive plastic surgery work was done in order to achieve looks like hers.

24) The Changing Face of Fame: Michael has reportedly had every plastic surgery procedure known to man done to him, including having a "scruffy look" beard applied to his face. He has used chemical bleaching agents for years that lighten his skin, even though these chemical agents are reputed to be highly carcinogenic. In addition, he has had countless facial peels to remove the scars of teenaged acne. He wants to be a whiter shade of pale and often wears a white facial cream that looks like something left over from Emmett Kelly's old makeup kit.

25) Flying Like Peter Pan: Michael said about his Peter Pan obsession: "We can fly, you know. We just don't think the right thoughts and levitate ourselves."

26) Fighting with the "Heifer": After a spat in which Madonna learned that Jackson had referred to her as "heifer," the singer responded: "I'd rather look like a cow than a space alien drag queen."

27) Michael Jackson, Freak: Michael Jackson once said, "When I'm not onstage, I sort of close down." Without question he is an adrenaline junky who can't handle normal life. He needs excitement at all times. He has gone so far as to state, fatally in terms of his downfall, that the only other time, besides being onstage, when he feels complete and fully alive, is when he's at play with young children. He needs intense drama to the brink of frenzy. So, during performance downtime, when normal, boring, routine life intrudes, he acts bizarre.

The reason?

He's the oddest and most outlandish creature on earth — a FREAK!

ACKNOWLEDGMENTS

The author would like to thank the reporters, researchers and editors of the National Enquirer, Star and Globe. Thanks go out, as well, to Michael Jackson for *Moonwalk*, to LaToya Jackson for *LaToya: Growing Up in the Jackson Family*, to Christopher Andersen for *Michael Jackson: Unauthorized*, to Lois P. Nicholson for *Michael Jackson: Entertainer*, to J. Randy Taraborrelli for *Michael Jackson: The Magic and the Madness* and to Quincy Jones for *Q*.